# Celebrations of Biblical Women's Stories
# Tears, Milk, and Honey

Martha Ann Kirk, CCVI
with songs by Colleen Fulmer

Sheed & Ward

Abreviations:
JB for Jerusalem Bible
NAB for New American Bible

*The New American Bible*, Thomas Nelson, P. O. Box 141000, Nelson Place at Elm Hill Pike, Nashville, Tn. 37214

*The Jerusalem Bible*, Doubleday & Co., Inc., 245 Park Ave., New York, New York 10017

*Southern Exposure*, Institute of Southern Studies, P. O. Box 531, Durham, N.C. 27702

Center Focus, Center of Concern, 3700 13th St., Washington, D.C. 20017

Parts of Chapter 2 and the two songs, "Washerwoman God" and the "Judge's Dilemma" have appeared in articles that I wrote for Modern Liturgy, 160 E. Virgina St. #290, San Jose, Ca. 95112

Seven of the stories can be heard on *God of Our Mothers: Seven Biblical Women Tell Their Stories* cassette tapes, St. Anthony Messenger Press, 1615 Republic St., Cincinnati, Ohio 45210

Sheed & Ward ™ is a service of National Catholic Reporter Publishing Company, Inc.

Library of Congress Catalog Card Number: 87-62678

ISBN:1-55612-097-4

Published by: Sheed & Ward
115 E. Armour Blvd. P.O. Box 414292
Kansas City, MO 64141-4292

To order, call: (800) 333-7373

# Contents

# Acknowledgments

I am grateful to the Sisters of Charity of the Incarnate Word, my parents Ada and Bert Kirk, Robbi, Cindy, Meredith and Morgen Kirk, Doug Adams, Edwina Hunter, Michael E. Moynahan, S.J., and Antoinette Clark Wire, Theresa Kobak, Maria Teresa Flores; and the members of the Loretto Spirituality Network, especially the core: Kathleen Tighe, Kay Lane, Klarise Davis, and Harriet Dow with whom many of the celebrations were shared. I am endebted to my creative and sensitive sister Colleen Fulmer, who collaborated by creating music and my prayerful brother Rufino Zaragoza, O.F.M. Conv., who so often supported me with music. These celebrations were born as part of a dissertation which was greatly encouraged by the Center for Women and Religion at the Graduate Theological Union in Berkeley. Cindy Winton-Henry and the members of the Graduate Theological Union Community Dancers stimulated me and danced with me. I appreciate Mary Schmidt, Coral nunnery, the many people who have helped develop these celebrations, and the thousands of people who have prayed with me, and often shared their reflections as I tried to refine these celebrations. I have felt the Spirit moving and dancing through all these companions along the way.

# LIST OF ILLUSTRATIONS

1. *"Rechem,"* by Martha Ann Kirk, CCVI
Photography: Don Ewers

2. "Our Lady of the Sign," by Martha Ann Kirk, CCVI

3. Creator God, fertile womb of all, the rock who bore us
Photography: Cindy Winton-Henry

4. Will a mother forget her infant, be without tenderness for the child of her womb?
Photography: Cindy Winton-Henry

5. As a mother comforts her child, so will I comfort you
Photograpahy: Cindy Winton-Henry

6. I led them with reins of kindness
Photography: Cindy Winton-Henry

7. "How Often Have I Longed to Gather You....," by Martha Ann Kirk, CCVI

8. "Sometimes I feel like a motherless child"
Photography: Cindy Winton-Henry

9. Miriam took a tambourine and led the people in praise
Photography: Cindy Winton-Henry

10. Our God wants freedom for all
Photography: Don Ewers

11. Will we ever reach the promised land?
Photography: Dale Rott

12. Sample program for the service
Photography: Al Rendon

13. Where did you get this stuff of calling the "apostle to the apostles" a loose woman?
Photography: Dave Moynahan

14. The bread and wine are brought to the table
Photography: Dave Moynahan

15. Pour out upon us the Spirit of the Risen Christ that we may dance though we are in bondage
Photography: Dave Moynahan

16. May we, like Mary, go forth and proclaim that Christ is alive
Photography: Dave Moynahan

17. Let us reclaim the circle dance of a discipleship of equals
Photography: Don Ewers

18. Let us gather in a circle
by Martha Ann Kirk, CCVI

# Chapter I

# Tears, Milk, and Honey

One of the oldest passages in the bible says that the prophetess Miriam picked up a tambourine and led the people in dance and praise of God. They celebrated because they were moving away from bondage toward a promised land of freedom and justice. Celebrations are still needed, for God's people continue the journey away from bondage toward a promised land flowing with milk and honey. As the bondage of racism, materialism, militarism, and sexism continue, the proclamation of prophecy, the abandonment of dance, and the power of praise are all the more urgently needed. The people on the way need ancient stories to assure them that people survive the journey. They need new stories to give them visions of the land to come that they may not grow weary and lose heart. New stories can be found in the ancient stories. The voice of the Spirit cries out in the fragments of the often forgotten or sometimes suppressed words of Miriam and her sisters through the ages.

Elisabeth Schussler Fiorenza, the biblical theologian, defines four areas in which women's perspectives are needed. In *Bread Not Stone,* which expresses the hope that God's word may be "bread not stone" for women, she speaks of (1) a hermeneutics of suspicion, (2) a hermeneutics of remembrance and historical reconstruction, (3) a hermeneutics of proclamation, (4) a hermeneutics of ritualization and celebration. In the hermeneutics of ritualization, historical imagination and artistic recreation are used. The remnants of women's experiences that have survived in patriarchal texts are reclaimed and elaborated. The church of the past in liturgy, art, and midrash has celebrated the "founding fathers." Today "founding mothers" need to be celebrated also. Fiorenza suggests that creative celebrations of our forgotten sisters can be the leaven of bakerwoman God that can transform traditional Christianity into good bread for those who seek liberation from oppression.[1]

The United Nations' *State of the World's Women 1985,* a publication prepared for the Nairobi gathering of women to close the U.N. Decade of Women, said that women do most of the domestic work throughout the world. Very many of them also work outside the home which means that most women work a double day. Women grow about half of the world's food, but own hardly any land. Thus it is difficult for them to get loans and legal protection, benfits, or aid. Women are one-third of the world's official labor force, but are concentrated in the lowest paid occupations and are more vulnerable to unemployment than men. Women still receive less than three-quarters of the wage of men doing similar work. There are three females to every two males among the world's illiterate. Ninety percent of the nations in the world have started organizations promoting the advancement of women. Yet since women have had poorer education, because they lack confidence, and because they have greater workloads, women are still dramatically under-represented in the decision-making bodies of their countries.[2]

One should not think that everything is good for men and bad for women. Men do not live as long as women, and they are more prone to disease, accidents, childhood emotional disorders, alcoholism and drug addiction.[3] Men commit more than 90 percent of major violent crimes and burglaries and 100 percent of the rapes. They are 94 percent of the drunken drivers and 91 percent of the offenders against family and children.[4] In citing these statistics on men the intention is not to indicate that women are morally better than men. Each gender is victim in different ways. However, these statistics on women and on men do indicate that gender is a significant category. To act as if human personhood were the same for both genders is to deny reality. To deny the differences between genders perpetuates the problems, and to allow men to speak for women in the world and in the church perpetuates the problems.

Statistics represent people with the tears wiped off.[5] Cold, empirical studies can hide the tears, dissect the figures, trends, relationships, and causes; but transformation is needed to wipe away the tears. Scripture tells us that our loving God comes to wipe away tears from people's eyes. God comes so that there shall be no more death or mourning, crying out or pain (Rev.

21:4). God comes to make a New Creation in which there is to be neither "male nor female" (Gal. 3:28). This book is a collection of prayers—prayers turning to God to wipe away the tears of the women of the world, that they may continue to wipe away others' tears. Scripture is proclaimed to announce that there is more than bad news. Persons who suffer today are not alone, a cloud of witnesses before has endured suffering. Yet, scripture offers more than models of suffering endured. God's word offers the power to name and confront evil, the power to leave behind a land of bondage and seek a land of freedom, and the possibility of death itself being transformed into life.

Where and to what extent are women a part of the biblical story? Scholars search for the "real words" of Jesus in the midst of the communities', authors', and editors' retelling, embellishment, and editing of those words. Scholars are more and more searching for the "real words" of women in scriptural texts which have obviously been reshaped by the patriarchal perspectives of communities, authors, and editors. As I became aware of this search for women's words, I could identify with the words of Antoinette Clark Wire who wrote that since her people—that is, the women—were largely illiterate in the early Christian period, she began to focus on the stories told rather than just the literary works.[6] The telling needs primary consideration. These celebrations have focused on women as oral storytellers in a folk style with folk music and dance. This seemed an appropriate way to relate to biblical women. Their major influence was in the oral and folk traditions. The partial loss of biblical women's expressions within written texts and the academy could be compared to the loss of women's "folk arts" of doll-making, quilt-making and storytelling while men's painting, sculpture, and writings have been preserved in the study of American fine art.

Today, there is speculation about women's words in the first two chapters of Exodus, some of the psalms with feminine images, the Song of Songs, the women's canticles (Miriam, Deborah, Judith, Hannah), Ruth, Mark, and Hebrews.[7] Perhaps women storytellers, evangelizers, and prophets gave content to Luke and the Johannine author. Yet, even if all this speculation were true, the amount of women's speech and stories in relation to men's would still be a very small fraction of the biblical heritage. Women are almost wordless, but the real dilemma is that from generation to generation very few people have seemed to notice or question this. The situation is as unquestioned as the system of slavery for about four thousand years. Speech is a primary characteristic of the human being. When the speech of a group is not heard, that group can unconsciously be thought of and related to as less than human.

Edwina Hunter, in a sermon to celebrate the publication of *An Inclusive Language Lectionary*, spoke of what it has meant for women to be almost hidden through the sexist language patterns within biblical texts and translations. She said that it has been like the footbinding that Chinese women endured for centuries. Women have been spiritually bound and crippled. Discovering feminine images of God is like being unbound.[8] Discovering strong women role models is like being unbound. At first it can be painful and hard to walk, but finally it is wonderful and one can learn to dance with God, our sister, and sisters through the centuries.

Before people make stories, they listen to stories. The child is mainly who she is told she is. With growth comes awareness and freedom to choose stories, to choose identity, to choose self. People need stories that affirm them and give them security. Such stories bring consolation and joy. Also stories that challenge false securities are necessary. When stories break down false securities, they can be called soteriological or liberating stories. The movement from one stage of storytelling to another stage, which involves a threat to the person's sense of security, is the basic process of human development. What signals development at another level is the ability to tell stories in new ways.

Liturgy has been the primary context in which the Christian story has been told for the people of God. The Christian story, basically the paschal mystery, is retold, varied, amplified and deepened in the innumerable stories used within rituals, both those read in the lectionary and those used in interpreting them. The Christian story is also told in the symbolic language of the content and the style of performing the rituals.

Religious peoples through the ages have used ritual contexts to explore and keep alive their sacred stories. A ritual context makes a story more authoritative and reinforces its symbols and themes through texts, music, actions and environment. The word has been given flesh. Ritual deals with the bodily, with what is known through sight, touch, taste, smell, and hearing. Not just the mind but the whole body is involved in ritual. Ritual moves its participants beyond the cognitive domain. Ritual focuses attention and deepens perception. One comes to "know" more than can be transmitted by words.

Rituals limit or expand one's possibilities. Though ritual and mysticism can seem like escapes from the reality of social problems, authentic Christian ritual and mysticism are not. Rather they are contexts for gaining perspective and clarity from which Christians return with a deeper commitment to justice and charity. In *The Ritual Process*, Victor Turner, wrote that rituals can expand peoples possibilities. In rituals, carnivals, dramas, films, and other liminal experiences, people are open to a play of thoughts, feelings, and will. In these situations, new models of social and political relationships can be generated. Turner notes the possibility within ritual for transformation; in this subjunctive mood, in this liminal space and time, new things become possible.[9] Yet, at the same time, ritual can also be understood as a force that prevents change, that stabilizes, that promotes the status quo. Religious rituals are like speech forms in that they are transmitters of culture, which by their selections and emphases can shape people's belief and behavior. The social relationships within a group are communicated and reinforced through ritual. Religious rituals can give divine sanction to the structure of social relationships. A change in the symbolic language of the ritual can indicate divine sanction of other relationships. In other words, ritual opens up people's imaginations and makes new possibilities.

Women's experiences (birthing, nurturing, healing) are main metaphors of the sacred in Christian rituals which have traditionally been led by men. Women find much of the sacred in their own biology; often they have not needed to go outside of themselves to find God. In rites of initiation in primitive societies, boys' initiation was an introduction into a world that was not immediate, a world of spirit and culture. For girls, initiation involved a series of revelations of the sacred meaning of a natural phenomenon, their sexual maturity and reproductive capacity.[10] This discussion does not mean aboriginal religions and Christianity are just alike in the relationships between gender and religious activity, yet some similarity can be seen. Women have not written on the transcendent as much as men, but women have not needed to do so because the divine has been so apparent in the immanence of their reproductive cycles and in the intimate relationships they have had with children and others for whom they have cared. While men cannot have children, they can have intimate relationships and be caretakers. The sacred is discovered in such relationships and care. This encounter with the sacred may be an even more profound encounter than that "power" to invoke the sacred conferred with ordination. Men in their theology and rituals need to explore the sacred in human relationships, nurturing, and caretaking (the footwash-

ing of which Jesus spoke), instead of dwelling on the fact that the "power" to perform the rituals has been given them. Women in their theology and rituals need to realize and celebrate that they do have the power of the sacred among them because they have known all along the skills of relationships, nurturing, and caretaking.

The biblical women dealt with in these celebrations say very little within recorded scripture, but their bodies or their concern for the care of other's bodies are important. While in most of the rituals the biblical women speak, the bodily involvement in the rituals is as important as the verbal content. The medium, as well as the text, conveys the message. Women's part in salvation history has focused on their bodies. While efforts at including women in worship have often been efforts for women to form their minds and function as men, the effort in these celebrations is to create rituals celebrating the women's bodies, as well as their words. This feminine, bodily worship is not a lower order than masculine, intellectual worship, it is an authentic aspect of the incarnation and of a creation-centered spirituality.

Women are not merely bodies, but women with their female bodiliness have something to contribute to culture and religion. These celebrations explore bodiliness in many ways: All of the rituals involve dance and all involve touching, eating, drinking, or anointing. Sarah had a body which was barren, but finally fruitful. Hagar had a fruitful body which was then rejected. Miriam led the people in dance, bodily prayer. Susanna's body was to be exploited. Though Naomi had brought forth children, her body seemed to be fruitless because of their death. She and Ruth collaborated about how Ruth could use her body to allure another and to carry on the family. Though it is not clear what is meant by casting seven demons out of Mary of Magdala, she seems to have been freed from a spiritual, emotional or physical disease. In Mark 5, the bleeding woman longed for her body to be cured, and the daughter had her body restored to life. Martha was concerned with the bodily needs of others. Dorcas' ministry was to clothe the bodies of the needy.

The feminine body is used as a primary metaphor for God. God's compassion is like a sheltering womb. People are God-like in giving birth. Mary gave an example of giving birth for people to follow. Hagar seeks a "sister" God to teach her and Sarah how to live as sisters and not rivals. Hagar seeks a "mother" God to understand her cries as a mother. Miriam speaks of God who writhes in labor pains to give birth and a God whose compassion is revealed in the midwives who assist at birth.  Miriam describes God who, like a woman, sees that her wandering family has food, water, and clothing.  Ruth knows the God of Israel through her mother-in-law, and that God is the one under whose wings she seeks shelter.  The story of Susanna, who will not let herself be exploited, is used with the story of the widow who persistently demands justice from the judge.  In song and dance God is compared to the widow who persistently knocks at the hard hearts of people.  Martha speaks of daughters, filled with the Spirit, who prophesy.  These women are the voice of, and in some way personify, the Spirit.

One of the major things learned in the process of sharing these stories and celebrations with over ten thousand people in many different groups over a period of years is the great need for imagination and humor in worship that seeks justice.  Most of the stories began as "serious reflections" on "serious topics."  While my early homilies involved explaining feminist exegesis, I slowly began to develop imaginative stories grounded in the exegesis.  Good stories cannot be explained.  One enters into them and experiences them.  The beauty and mystery of story is that many people can identify with stories in many different ways, as Michael E. Moynahan has pointed out.[11]  Imagination captures people's hearts in ways that explanation fails to do.  In George Bernard Shaw's play *Saint Joan*, Robert, the lord from whom Joan seeks aid, is a skeptic about the voices which Joan hears.  She says that the messages come from God.  Robert responds that they come from her imagination.  She firmly explains that certainly they come from her imagination—that is the way God's messages come to us.

Imagination has invited people to live in these stories about the past which are actually stories about the future.  In story and ritual one is removed from chronological or linear time with past, present, and future and immersed in chiarotic or graced time which participates in God's eternity.  The obstacles and idols of the present lose their power in this open realm.

Doug Adams indicates that in worship and preaching humor has been one of the most effective ways to exorcise idolatries, particularly idolatries of political and ecclesiastical power and pretensions of wisdom.[12]  These celebrations exorcise some of the idolatry of patriarchy within Christian worship.  Yet, the idolatry of feminism as the savior of the world is exorcised as well.  The arts and humor, far from being frivolous and irrelevant, give prophets the clarity and strength to remain faithful to inner truth and not be captivated by idols equivalent to those of the oppressors.  The arts confuse our simple categories of oppressor and oppressed and give us a glimpse of God's sun which shines on all.  Humor does not detract from communicating the poignancy or pain of the stories.  In fact, humor keeps the audience close enough to the characters to be open to the characters' feelings.  Comic relief has been used in tragic dramas through the centuries to intensify the stories. Humor creates a rapport that can be stronger than barriers people put up to protect themselves from the painful.

Christianity needs worship with liturgical arts informed by prophecy (political awareness), in contrast to political propaganda masquerading as worship.  This political propaganda can take the form of such things as a current Sunday Roman Ritual with over sixty male metaphors.[1]

Ritual is liminal activity similar to play.  People who have reduced Christianity to moralism have identified worship with teaching dogma or morality and reduced participation in worship to fulfilling a moral obligation.  The celebrations of this book do not "fulfill an obligation" and their open-ended stories do not give dogma and morality.  The leadership of the rituals has not been defined by the game rules of any religious institution.  In the field of leisure and recreation, an area of "new games" is developing which searches for new types of play that encourage people to be supportive, cooperative and open with each other.  Most of our traditional games have ignored or positively broken down self-confidence.[13]  In *Playfair: Everybody's Guide to Noncompetitive Play* new ways to play and some of the important characteristics of a play facilitator are given.  A play facilitator believes in the abilites of all the players, builds their confidence and cooperation.  People are often "afraid of looking silly," and a facilitator helps them to overcome these inhibitions through her or his sense of playfuless and willingness to take risk. The facilitator blends structure and flexibility.[14]

Most traditional games in Western society have not built people's self-confidence. Traditional Catholic rituals frequently have not built the self-confidence of females or other marginal peoples.  Less than ten percent of the readings used in the Roman Catholic lectionary give stories of women, and the stories used usually deal with women being helped or saved, rather than as being strong or competent in themselves.  The rituals of this book endeavor to give women and marginal people self-confidence.  The desirable characteristics of a play facilitator mentioned above, rather than the "rules" of how to lead traditional Christian worship have been the guiding factors.

When children and adults play new games together everyone is a peer, playmates are equal not hierarchical.[15] There are leaders in the celebrations of this book, but the leaders model storytellers among peers who speak to evoke other stories (which are equally God's revelation), rather than preachers from high pulpits giving eternal truth to the people. While the celebrations here spell out directions and texts for prayers, these are only meant as suggestions and springboards. Flexibility and creativity are most desirable.

At the Last Supper, Peter was upset when Jesus wanted to wash the disciples' feet. Peter had not minded when Jesus healed people, fed them, or did other things. Footwashing confused hierarchical structure; it confused masters and servants. Today "power with" rather than "power over" is needed in our world. Both in biblical culture and today it is more common for women to wash children, the sick, and the elderly, than for men to wash others. Women washing feet can be an act of kindness but it does not necessarily reverse roles of power as Jesus' action did. When women, whose voices have not been heard telling their own stories in the church or in the world, speak up, it is radical activity like Jesus washing feet. This may change in the future, but today it seems that speech is for women as footwashing is for men.

Within these celebrations everyone dancing has been one the most important parts. The whole atmosphere of these rituals has created both a safe and a transforming space. The early Jesus movement had been a discipleship of equals. In the early Christian communities people had danced in circles saying that this mirrored the angels dancing around the throne of God, but as clergy divided themselves from and put themselves above laity in the fourth and fifth century circle dancing was suppressed as too equalizing and revolutionary.[16] Circle dancing has been one of the most powerful and healing parts of these celebrations binding up dualisms of soul and body, reason and emotion, male and female. The Word becomes flesh, the Word becomes dance.

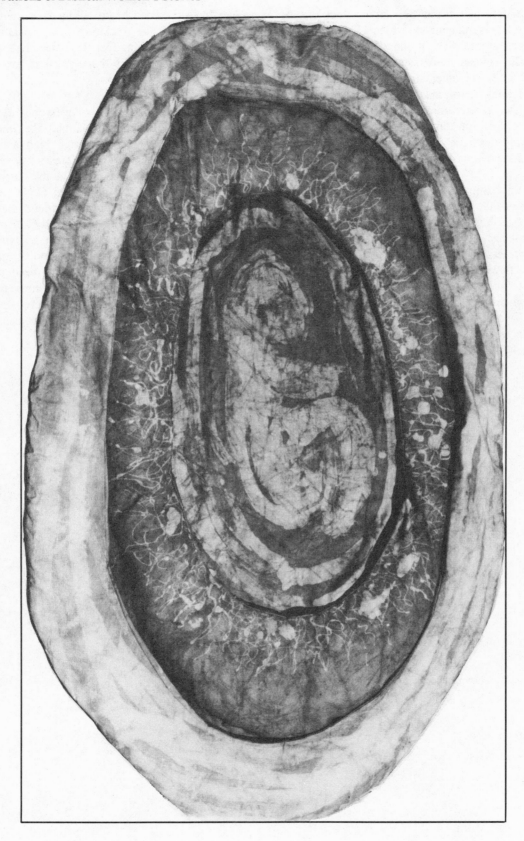

Illustration 1: "*Rechem*," by Martha Ann Kirk, CCVI

# Chapter 2

# God Who Mothers and Teaches Us to Mother

## Themes

• Being born and giving birth

• Compassion and tenderness of mothering

• Overcoming fear

• Openness to new possibilities

## Possible Uses

• Advent

• Feasts of Mary such as the Annunciation, the Visitation, and the Immaculate Conception

• Baptismal preparation programs and pregnancy support groups

• Justice programs on caring for children and for the hungry

## The Service

(This service may be done with chairs in an oval shape with openings at each end. We have used art pieces at each end of the oval. If the service is done in a church with a traditional arrangement of pews, the art pieces and the table can be in the front. At one side where the first part of the dance is done, there is a womblike soft-sculpture image; at the other end, there is a large icon design of Christ in the womb of Mary. In the center, there is a table with a cloth and candles which will be lighted within the service.)

Presider: You are invited to get in groups of two or three and share brief stories of pregnancy and birth that are special for you. (People share for a few minutes.)

Let us in silence cherish these stories in our hearts for a few moments as we prepare to pray.

(The following explanation could be printed in a program and/or the presider could give the explanation.)

**Presider:** We are called to be compassionate as our loving God is compassionate. The Hebrew word for compassion, *rachamim,* is from the same root word as the word meaning womb, *rechem.*[1] God's compassion is like a womb in which we are created, nourished, and healed, and in which we can grow strong. Let us pray that we may experience and share compassion. What is probably the oldest image of Mary the mother of Jesus, a picture in a second-century catacomb, shows her in the early Christians' position of prayer, that is, with open arms. This gesture, called the *orans* position, the Christians explained as showing their attitude of openness to God. The gesture reflected Jesus who opened his arms in love on the cross, a gesture open to embrace all. This was also a Jewish position of prayer. Mary with open arms has the unborn Christ in her womb shining through, a transfiguration within her. May we nurture Christ within us as faithfully as a mother nurtures life within herself. (Pause after the explanation.)

**Presider:** Let us rise and pray in joyful hope. (Pauses, then opens arms to an *orans* position and continues. Throughout this a large icon of Mary with open arms in prayer, the *orans* position, is visible as an example of not only a gesture but an attitude of prayer.) Loving God, we prepare for you; and yet we know you are among us. We call you Father, but we know you are just as much our Mother. We ask for your light, and yet you are just as truly in the darkness. May we not fear the darkness. May darkness be like the sheltering creative darkness of the womb, your womb of compassion, in which our life is nurtured and grows strong. We ask this through Jesus who waited in the creative darkness of Mary's womb. And we pray in the power of the Holy Spirit who guides us forever and ever. Amen. (The presider gestures for all to be seated. The song "Rachamim," by Colleen Fulmer, which may be found in the Appendix, is sung.)

**First Reader:** Readings and reflections from Isaiah 40, 49, and 66; Hosea 11; and Luke 2.

(Silent pause...soft soothing music begins. From three to eight dancers at different levels, some squatting, some bent over, and some standing, are in a circular cluster. Very slowly, the dancers begin breathing, undulating up and down, and gently swaying.)

Illustration 2: "Our Lady of the Sign," by Martha Ann Kirk, CCVI

Illustration 3: Creator God, fertile womb of all, the rock who bore us

Illustration 4: Will a mother forget her infant, be without tenderness for the child of her womb?

Illustration 5: As a mother comforts her child, so will I comfort you

**First:** Creator God, fertile womb of all, the rock who bore us.[2]

**Second:** You formed us in our mothers' wombs, and you are like a mothering womb.[3]

**First:** (Starting in a whisper and building as a rhythmic chant.) Womb of compassion, rachamim, rachamim, womb of compassion, rachamim, rachamim, rachamim....[4]

**Second:** (Same chant effect.) Compassion, compassion, compassion....

(The rachamim and the compassion chant overlap and intermingle as the dancers are "born." One at a time, the dancers come pushing out of the tight cluster from the bottom. They move out in different directions reaching and fearfully exploring the strange space. They are like newborns in an unknown world.)

**First:** Will a mother forget her infant, be without tenderness for the child of her womb? Yet, even if she forgets, I will never forget you. I have carved you on the palm of my hand.[5]

(The dancers move with more confidence and venture out farther.)

**Second:** As mother comforts her child, so will I comfort you.[6]

**First:** I myself took them in my arms; yet they have not understood that I was the one looking after them.

(The dancers start to go to each other and lead, help, and caress each other. Slowly, they are moving toward the center area.)

**First:** I led them with reins of kindness, with leading-strings of love. I was like someone who holds an infant close.[7]

(The dancers should come to the front and hold still.)

**Second:** "Comfort my people, O comfort them," God says to us through the prophet Isaiah.[8] We recall that God sees our needs, wishes to comfort us, and teaches us to comfort others. Let us hold hands as a way of sharing God's comforting touch. (A pause as the congregation holds hands and the dancers hold hands.)

**First:** Let us express our prayers of gratitude for the ways we feel God's touch, and let us pray for those who need God's creative compassionate embrace.

(As members of the congregation spontaneously pray, the dancers improvise movements embodying the sentiments expressed. When these are finished, the dancers stand still.)

**First:** Loving God, you hear our prayers as you heard the prayers of your people Israel. We know you are near.

(The dancers drop hands and face the table. This is a cue to the congregation that they may drop hands. The chorus and a verse of the song, "Rachamim," is repeated.)

**Second:** Wake, wake. May our lamps be lit. Let us prepare and adorn ourselves as Jerusalem, the mother of God's people preparing for the Savior.

(Two dancers quietly start lighting candles on the table. About two dozen candles of different shapes and sizes asymmetrically placed can be attractive. Soft music may be used. The music starts to get lower and the dancers move toward the sanctuary area. They should look excited and assume a pose of looking into the far distance, watching and waiting for the one who is to come. The music finishes.)

**First:** And when the time had come for God's plan to be fulfilled....In the sixth month, the angel Gabriel was sent from God to a town of Galilee named Nazareth, to a virgin betrothed to a man named Joseph, of the house of David. The virgin's name was Mary. Upon arriving the angel said to her: "Rejoice, O highly favored daughter! The Lord is with you. Blessed are you among women."

**Second:** She was deeply troubled by his words.

(One at a time the dancers move in fear to the far ends of the church. Some back away, some run, some go hesitantly. They try to protect themselves. They go into corners and huddle against the walls. All are gone and there is a dead silence.)

**First:** The angel went on to say, "Do not fear, Mary....You shall conceive and bear a son and give him the name Jesus."

**Second:** Do not fear, Mary.

(A soft percussive beat starts. The words are like a chant that rises and falls.)

**First:** Do not fear. Fear not. Fear not. (The dancers begin to loosen up and slowly move out of hiding.) Do not fear, Moses. Do not fear, Miriam.

**Second:** Linda, Jim, Cathy, Doug, fear not. Jeremiah, do not fear. Isaiah, fear not. Henry, fear not.

**First:** Shirley, Susan, Sarah, do not fear. (Both readers continue mentioning names of people there.)

**Second:** Dale, Sue, Don, Ann, do not fear, do not fear. (The names begin to fade away. Then the percussive beat fades.)

**First:** *You* shall conceive and bear a son and give him the name Jesus.

(The dancers who are near the front but still in the midst of the congregation stare intensely at persons in the congregation as if saying, "*You* shall conceive." The dancers freeze like this.)

**Second:** (This is said timidly as one who is afraid but trying to cooperate, then the following prayers should lead into a full affirmation.) Yes—let it be done as you say.

(The dancers go and stand by the art piece of Mary with open arms, but they have fists clenched and they are bent over and closed in.)

**First:** If we are closed he cannot come; if we have built our walls, locked our doors, encased our hearts....

**Second:** Let us pray together in gesture and words, "Open our hands, open our hearts, Word become flesh among us."

(The dancers and the whole congregation repeat the words first opening their hands, then their arms. After it is finished, arms are dropped to the sides.)

**Second:** Let us pray aloud for those persons and situations which need Christ's redemptive presence. (People spontaneously pray for needs and after each petition the gesture and words are repeated.)

**First:** Then the angel left Mary.[9] (Pause, then the reader lifts the gospel book and says:) This is the good news.

(Colleen Fulmer's song "Blest Is She Who Believes," found in the Appendix, is sung.)

**Presider:** We are all one family. Let us gather close around the table of God; let us gather in union with God's faithful people through the ages.

(The congregation comes around the table and a pitcher of milk and honey and a basket of bread are brought to the table.)

**Presider:** Like hungry children around a mother's table, we gather with open hands. Despite our impatient clamor....

**First:** "Give us bread *now*."

**Presider:** You, God, pause and focus our eyes on other faces around the table. All of us are your children....

**Second:** Children of Lebanon, Louisiana, Guatemala, Alaska....

Illustration 6: I led them with reins of kindness

**First:** Children of South Africa, and North Dakota, Cambodia, El Salvador, Ohio, of New Jersey, Idaho, Ireland, Afghanistan....

**Presider:** Some with full hearts and empty stomachs, others stomach-full and empty-hearted. Some children grab for bread, others have too little strength even to reach. Beginning to see each other, we cry....

**Second:** "You will not leave us orphans?"

**First:** "Be without tenderness for the children of your womb?"

**Presider:** *Rachamim, rachamim,* compassion, *rachamim,* compassion,

O loving God, embrace us in your re-creating compassion.

We are your children born of water, born of Spirit.[10]

Teach us to break this bread in enough pieces for all the reaching hands, toil-worn hands....

**Second:** For the shriveled hands, strong hands, fragile hands....

**First:** For all the opening, grasping, stretching hands.

**Presider:** May this bread of seeds of the earth be planted as seed of heaven in our hearts. Jesus-life, grow in us. Show in us. Transfigure us within. Be born of us that we may be born.

(The presider and others begin breaking the bread.)

**Presider:** We share milk recalling that milk comes from within, that we have a milk of wisdom to share. We have substance within ourselves to nourish. We share milk and honey remembering that God promised us a land flowing with milk and honey where all might live in peace and joy. May we hear the cries of all who need nourishment and all who need sweetness.

(The presider holds up the bread, milk and honey, and says:)

Let us share these with each other praying that we may learn to compassionately share with all the human family.

(These are passed around the circle and all sing "Rachamim" again or the chant "Gentle loving God, the Mother of my soul, hold me as Your own," from *Chants for Meditation*, by Rufino Zaragoza, O.F.M. Conv. [National Catholic Reporter, P. O. Box 281, Kansas City, MO 64141]. People may be seated.)

**Presider:** Let us rise and stretch out our hands, reaching toward those in the world who particularly need God's blessing and pray for this. (Pause as all stretch out their hands.) Let us answer, "Amen."

We have been nurtured by your life and compassion. May we nurture all who hunger. Amen.

Jerusalem, your holy city prepares for redemption which is at hand. May we participate in renewing our cities as those who believe that your reign is among us. Amen.

Mary cooperated in your surprising plan of salvation. May we overcome all fear as she did and creatively bring forth your Word. Amen.

May the blessing of our loving God, Creator, Son, and Spirit, be with us forever. Amen.

## For Further Reflection, Journalizing, and/or Discussion

Scriptural Background: Luke 1:26-56

### Questions

1. What are some of your feelings about physical birth and other kinds of birth? Does birth seem sacred to you? In what ways have you given birth? Have you been afraid of giving birth?

2. Do you ever care for infants or small children? What have you learned about God from these experiences?

3. Have you ever wished to be really open to God, but when an invitation occurs, as the angel's invitation to Mary, you have become afraid?

4. How does Mary, in giving birth, image God who gave birth to creation?

5. Make a list of as many images of God as you can. For instance, God is like a light, like a sister, like a gentle breeze, like a mother, like laughter, like hope, like refreshing water. What feminine images or activities of God touch and inspire you?

### Readings

God's image (Gen. 1:27)

God is like:

• a nursing mother (Num. 11:12-13; Isa. 49:15)

• a woman giving birth (Deut. 32:18; Isa. 42:14)

• a midwife (Isa. 66:9; Ps. 22:10-11)

• a mother bird sheltering her young under her wings (Ruth 2:12; Ps. 17:8, 57:2, 61:5, and 91:4; Matt. 23:27; Luke 11:34)

• a mother eagle teaching her young to fly (Deut. 32:11; Exod. 19:4)

• one who prepares food and drink (Isa. 25:6; Wis. 16:20-21)

• one who cares for a little one (Isa. 46:3-4)

• one who sees that people are clothed (Gen. 3:21; Neh. 9:20-21; Luke 12:28)

• one who washes and cleans (Ps. 51:3-4; Ez. 36:25; John 3:5; Heb. 10:22)

• one who cares for a household (Ps. 123:1-2; Luke 15:8-10)

• one who takes care of a difficult child (Hos. 11:3-4)

• one who wipes away the tears of someone who is weeping (Isa. 25:8; Rev. 21:4)

## Reflections on the Development and Use of the Service

Mary is not just the passive figure dependent upon the active male, but an active partner with the divine, imaging the divine. The emphasis on overcoming fear in the section of the dance, based on Luke 2, has usually brought a good delightful laughter from those present. The divine becomes not a frightening figure above, but a companion with us, like us, giving us courage because the divine also has known the challenge of conception, the travail of labor pains, the burden of nurturing.

The dance was used in a service to bless a Women's Peace Delegation to Nicaragua. This women-to-women mission sought to protect all the children of the human family. This dance seemed to be expressive of their deep compassionate commitment. But the compassion seemed to be a "taken-for-granted" part of women's experience, the part of the dance that had particular power for the group and provoked the laughter of recognition, was the section, "Fear not.... do not fear...." The movement from running away, hiding, and cowering in fear, to an opening, growing, moving out, and finally a powerful, fast dance was highly significant for them. Can women, the bearers of life, overcome fear and take their places at the national and international tables where many of the life-preserving decisions are made?

In dancing this service, the whole group of dancers, which consists of women and men, have danced images of God giving birth, of humanity being born, of Mary open to conception, and of Mary bringing forth. The male dancers have spoken of what a moving experience it was for them to dance conception and giving birth. Many of us who have served as spiritual directors for men have noted that it is particularly powerful for men to identify with Mary because in this they can identify with a power of giving life which they do not have physically.

Birth involves strength, pain, and what might be called a "fierce tenderness." As we worked on the dance, we broke through some of our stereotypes of motherhood. Some of us had seen parts of Judy Chicago's art work, *The Birth Project*; its big, powerful, grounded women were far from the sweet images of mothers on pedestals so often seen on Mother's Day cards or in Catholic devotional art of Mary.

We knew stories of the "Mothers of the Disappeared" in countries of Latin America who defiantly protest governments which threaten the life from their wombs. Making a decision to bring to birth seemed a great act of courage. The improvisation of the dance grew in the contrast of natural emotions of fear overcome by great boldness to choose birth.

A variation of this service was shared at the National Women's Inter-Seminary Conference when people were being urged to boycott Nestle's products because the company extensively promoted their infant formula in the Third World countries. Women of these countries had previously nursed their off-spring. Mother's milk has medicinal qualities that often immunizes babies and protect them from disease. Studies indicate the significantly higher incidence of infant mortality in areas where mothers have been seduced by advertising to use formula rather than to nurse their babies. This service helped lead women into discussions of "trusting their own milk of inner wisdom," rather than being led to believe that "man-made milk" and male wisdom were better. This multinational exploitation seemed a metaphor for many ways women are led to depend on outside resources, instead of using their own significant inner resources.

# Chapter 3

# Sarah, Our Mother in Faith

## Themes

• Waiting and watching in ignorance

• Grieving because one is valued for what one can do, not for who one is

• The impossible being done through God

• Rejoicing in hope

## Possible Uses

• Advent, Feast of the Annunciation

• With lectionary readings of 18 to 24 December, which deal with pregnancy and birth; or with readings of the twelfth and thirteenth week in Ordinary Time, Cycle B

• With elderly people or with pregnancy-support groups

• To celebrate Abraham and Sarah as our parents in faith

## The Service

(Chairs are arranged in a semicircle with a table and a small stool toward the front. A cloth, candles, and flowers in colors related to the storyteller's clothing may be used on the table. "Sarah's Song" by Colleen Fulmer which is found in the Appendix is softly played or sung.)

**Presider:** Let us stand and pray. (Pause) God of our mothers and fathers, you called Sarah and Abraham to be your chosen people. This choice did not give them a position of privilege, but rather a chance to be instruments of your goodness to all. Peoples of the whole earth were to be blessed through them. You call us to be your chosen people. May we never use this election for power over others, but rather as an opportunity to be channels of your love, peace,

and justice, and joy for all. This we pray in the name of Jesus.

**All:** Amen.

(The presider gestures for all to be seated. If possible, invite an elderly man to be the first reader and an elderly woman to be the second reader.)

**First Reader:** A reading from the Book of Genesis.

**Second Reader:** Yahweh appeared to Abraham at the oak of Mamre while he was sitting by the entrance of the tent during the hottest part of the day. He looked up, and there he saw three men standing near him. As soon as he saw them, he ran from the entrance of the tent to meet them, and bowed to the ground.

**First:** "My lord, I beg you, if I find favor with you, kindly do not pass your servant by. A little water shall be brought; you shall wash your feet and lie down under the tree. Let me fetch a little bread and you shall refresh yourselves before going further."

**Second:** "Do as you say."

**First:** Abraham hastened to the tent to find Sarah. "Hurry, knead three bushels of flour and make loaves."

**Second:** They ate while he remained standing near them under the tree. "Where is your wife Sarah?"

**First:** "She is in the tent."

**Second:** "I shall visit you again next year without fail, and your wife will then have a son."

**First:** Sarah was listening at the entrance of the tent behind him. Now Sarah and Abraham were old, well on in years, and Sarah had ceased to have her monthly periods. So Sarah laughed to herself....

**Second:** "Now that I am past the age of childbearing, and my husband is an old man, is pleasure to come my way again?" (Pause)

**First:** Sarah bore Isaac. (Pause)

**Second:** It happened some time later that God put Abraham to the test. "Abraham, Abraham."

**First:** "Here I am."

**Second:** "Take your son, your only child Isaac, whom you love, and go to the land of Moriah. There you shall offer him as a burnt offering, on a mountain I will point out to you."

**First:** Rising early the next morning, Abraham saddled his ass and took with him two of his servants and his son Isaac. He chopped wood for the burnt offering and started on his journey to the place God had pointed out to him. On the third day Abraham looked up and saw the place in the distance [adapted from Gen. 18:1-14, 22:1- 4, JB].

**Second:** This is the word of God.

(The storyteller, perhaps wearing a loose-fitting colorful dress, walks in and looks out in the distance trying to see Abraham and Isaac. She has an anxious look on her face. She might carry a deep basket which has in the bottom the bread used later in the service. Occasionally, she sits on the small stool as she reminisces.)

**Storyteller:** "The trip to Moriah, the place of sacrifice, the place of vision, should take only six days, and yet Abraham and Isaac are not back yet. Abraham was so strange before they left. I asked where was the lamb for the sacrifice.[1] He would not talk, then finally he mumbled, 'God will provide.' Oh, how I know God provides—God provided us this wonderful child Isaac despite the impossibility. Our God laughs at impossibility. Yes, that is the child's name, Isaac—laughter— how our God laughs at impossibility. Is anything too marvelous for our God to do? God gave us this precious child. When God told Abraham that nations would come from us, my husband laughed and said, 'Can a child be born to a man who is a hundred years old? Or can Sarah give birth at ninety?'[2] Then, when we were living by the holy grove at Mamre, I heard the babble of the three strangers, 'This time next year your wife will have a child.' I said, 'Now that I am so withered and my husband is so old, am I still to have sexual pleasure?' and I laughed. One can either laugh or cry when one is overcome with grief. I choose to laugh.

"Perhaps I should say that my God has taught me to laugh in the face of grief, to laugh in the face of life. I couldn't always do that. God told Abraham to leave his homeland, but God gave no security of where he was to go. So Abraham took me and his possessions and started." [The next part invites humor.]

"My husband wandered to one place and then another—he said God was leading him, but he never knew where he was going. Maybe you know people like that? Again and again over the years, I had cried out to God.[3] When there was a famine, we went to the land of Egypt. I was young and beautiful then. Perhaps Abraham loved me, but I wondered. He was afraid that the Egyptians would want me, and that they would kill him to get me. To protect himself, his flocks and his property, he told me that I had to say that I was his sister. The pharaoh took me to his palace because he wanted me for a wife and sent flocks and herds, male and female slaves, asses, and camels to Abraham. I was terrified among these strange people. I cried out to God. God protected me. Pharaoh's house had severe plagues and they came to realize that taking me was the reason. Pharaoh was angry and said to Abraham, 'How could you do this to me?' I was sent back to Abraham.[4] And again when I was older, Abraham still wandered, this time to Negeb. Again, to protect himself he said that I was his sister and the ruler, Abimilech, took me to be a wife. He had a dream in which God told him not to touch me. Angered, he sent me back to Abraham, then Abimilech's family was healed, for God had closed the wombs of all of them because it was not right for me to be there.[5] I wanted to believe in God, a God gracious and compassionate who had promised that Abraham and I would be the parents of a great nation; yet, how could this be if Abraham sought his safety but would pass me off to others to protect himself? Did Abraham care about anyone other than himself? I searched for faith in God, I cried out to God." [She sits down.]

"God did bless us. God gave us a land flowing with milk and honey. God multiplied our flocks and our herds. But what is it to amass these and go to the grave unloved by human offspring? How I longed for a child, a little one to cradle in my arms, a son or even a daughter, to share our good fortune. Abraham wanted a son and though he could have easily taken another wife, he never did. When I felt all hope die in my womb, I offered Abraham my Egyptian slave, Hagar, to bear a child so that our home might not be empty.[6] I thanked God when she became pregnant, but then I felt so betrayed when she looked on me with disdain. I had no child of my own, and alas, a woman without a child counts for nothing among us. I was going to have sons through Hagar. I trusted her—even to share my husband's bed. Fruitless, frustrated, taunted, I could only cry.... Finally, I told Abraham to get rid of her and her child. The laws of my people say that a person like me has a right to do that when such a woman is looking down upon her mistress.[7]

"But before that, I cried, 'O God, now that I am old and gray, forsake me not.' Our God heard my prayers, our God answered, not by giving me life in my womb, but by teaching me how to laugh rather than to cry. People around me did not understand how or why a childless old woman could laugh. My God is a God of surprises. I learned to laugh as all natural hope was dead; I learned God was God. Not in children, not in wealth, not in prestige with Abraham, Hagar or anyone, but in God alone was my joy and my salvation." [She stands describing the scene.]

"Finally, one day, three strangers came to Mamre, where we lived near the trees and beauty sacred to me. We welcomed the strangers, though it was hot and we were tired. I made them fresh bread and we served them our finest food. They smiled at me and were grateful. What satisfaction it gave me to make and break bread for strangers—it is a blessing like the presence of God to be able to share a meal or to feed the hungry. God was there. Then, when I was standing in the entrance of the tent behind them, they said to Abraham, 'Next year without fail your wife will have a son.'"

[This part is said to invite laughter.] "Was this a way of complimenting a ninety-year-old woman who was spry enough to make such fine bread and prepare an instant banquet? I laughed so loud they heard me!" [She sits and slaps her knee as she laughs.]

"After that, weeks went by and my wrinkled stomach began to swell." [The humor continues.] "I was sick in the mornings, but sickness such as that brings laughter, not sorrow. Isaac came—pink, wrinkled, but certainly the most beautiful baby in the world—or do people always say that? He grows and our hope grows with him. Our God said, 'I will bless those who bless you....All the tribes of the earth shall bless themselves by you. I will be your God, you will be my people.' For Abraham and me, death is near, but our God is a God of life; our life goes on in Isaac." [She stands and agitatedly looks around.]

"Life? Life? Life goes on? Why aren't Abraham and Isaac back from the holy mountain? Is it that Abraham is too old to travel with any speed? Could he have fallen along the way? Could I go on if anything happened to Abraham? Or could something have happened to the child? Could he have wandered off alone and gotten lost? Did Abraham fear something like that could happen? Why was he so agitated before they left? Why wouldn't he talk to me about the sacrifice?

"The sun is down and they are still not home. It is getting dark and I'm cold." [She shivers or perhaps puts on a shawl. Then she looks up at the sky and points.] "There is a little star. 'Look up to heaven count the stars if you can. Such will be your descendants....' Yes, there is the first star."

(She sits waiting hopefully and perhaps gently rocks as "Sarah's Song" by Colleen Fulmer which may be found in the Appendix is sung. After this, the participants can be invited to write dialogues with Sarah in their spiritual journals or on paper that has been provided. If journalizing is not wanted, the readers may begin the period of shared prayers with these or other prayers.)

**First:** When all our natural hopes have died and we have no one and nothing but you in whom to delight, teach us to laugh rather than cry.

**Second:** When we prepare to sacrifice our sons and daughters to the deity war, may your angel hold back our hands and teach us what you really want.

**First:** When we wait alone in darkness, cold, and fear, teach us to see the stars and trust in your faithful love.

**Second:** You are invited to share your prayers, hopes and reflections.

(After some time for this, the presider invites all to join in a circle around the table. A loaf of bread is brought in or taken from Sarah's basket and placed on the table.)

**Presider:** God of stars, hopes, and dreams, we remember Sarah and Abraham, our parents in faith, and all who have come to know your faithful love. We remember Rebekah, Rachel, and Manoah who were at first barren. We remember Hannah and Elizabeth who, like Sarah, grew old with no offspring. Their stories give us, your daughters and sons, hope when all within us is shriveled and dead.

We remember the widow of Zarephath, who fed and cared for your prophet Elijah. We remember Abigail, who prepared food for David and his companions—her wisdom and nourishment preventing them from turning to violence. We remember Ruth, who gathered food for her elderly mother-in-law, Naomi. We remember Esther, who prepared a banquet for the king that she might have a chance to plead for her people's lives. Your faithful daughters who image you in nourishing their families outnumber the grains of sand upon the shore.

God of fruitfulness and nourishment, we commend to you all those who feed the hungry as we praise you for their example. Sisters and brothers, let us mention aloud those who have fed us and those who have fed the needy in the world. (People mention names such as Dorothy Day, Grandmother Kirk, Martin De Porres, Aunt Mag.)

God of surprises, Sarah and Abraham, like the couple on the road to Emmaus, shared bread with strangers and encountered you. You blessed them with Isaac to delight their hearts. We thank you for Jesus, who like Isaac brought laughter and hope. We remember Isaac, the only beloved son who was to be sacrificed, but his father's hand was stopped. We faintly hear of the daughter of Jephthah, the only beloved daughter, who was sacrificed by her father. "From year to year the daughters of Israel went to mourn for the daughter of Jephthah." Let us not forget her story and the many stories of your sacrificed daughters as we break this bread.

Fill us with your Spirit of Wisdom who makes a banquet and says, "Come eat my bread and drink the wine I have prepared." Your beloved child, Jesus, did not consider it beneath his dignity to feed the multitudes bread, to cook and serve fish to his surprised disciples on the shore, and more than this, to offer his very self as nourishment. He teaches us to value those who prepare food, and he teaches us to generously feed others. May we share this bread today re-committing ourselves to share with all who are hungry, to welcome strangers, and to tell the stories of faith.

(The bread is broken and passed around. All sing the chant "For You Alone My Soul in Silence Waits," by Rufino Zaragoza, O.F.M. Conv., from *Chants for Meditation* [*National Catholic Reporter*, P. O. Box 281, Kansas City, MO 64141].)

**Presider:** Loving God, we have been nourished and strengthened by your word, this food, and the cloud of witnesses around us. May these help us to be like Sarah—hospitable to strangers, strong in faith, and persevering in hope. This we ask in the name of Jesus. Amen.

Let us again join hands and sing and dance.

(The song "Ruah" by Colleen Fulmer, given in the Appendix, might be used.)

# For Further Reflection, Journalizing, and/or Discussion

Scriptural Background: Genesis 12, 15, 16, 18, 21, and 22

## Questions

1. Biblical women were valued as bearers of offspring, especially sons. Have you ever defined your value in terms of your ability to produce something? How do we define others' value in terms of their ability to produce?

2. Have you ever been confronted with your own limitations? Have you ever experienced the "God of surprises" who answers prayers in unexpected ways? Have you ever discovered that "God is God," and found joy in the discovery?

3. Have you ever experienced God's special presence in sharing food?

4. How can bringing situations out in the open for discussion and prayer help clarify them? Did Abraham have a right to act without Sarah's collaboration? How do mothers feel when leaders make decisions to sacrifice their children's lives and to wage war? How can we begin to listen to mothers' feelings and stories?

5. What symbols like Sarah's star give us hope in time of fear or difficulties? What symbols speak of God's faithfulness?

6. The writers of scripture explained fruitfulness as God's protection, compensation, or enrichment. Have you every experienced spiritual or physical fruitfulness in these ways? Have you found that God fruitfulness occurs in God's own time and way?

## Readings

Stories of special pregnancies:

• God consoles Leah since she is not loved (Gen. 29:31-35)

• Manoah, who is barren, has Samson (Judg. 13:2-24)

• Hannah's prayers are answered in Samuel (I Sam. 1:1- 2:11)

• The elderly Elizabeth has John (Luke 1:5-25)

• Mary, a virgin, conceives (Luke 1:26-38)

• While Isaac is not sacrificed, Jephthah's daughter is (Judg. 11:30-34)

• Blessing of God's presence in hospitality (Luke 24:13-35)

## Reflections on the Development and Use of the Service

Women listeners to this story of Sarah have often identified with the challenge of following one's husband from place to place. Today, it is more common for spouses to mutually decide where to live based on opportunities for both parties. Yet, I have asked many groups with whom I have used this story if their places of residence were mutually determined by the parents or if the wife followed the husband's job. The large majority has experienced the wife following the husband both in this generation and the last generation. Sarah's questions about following her husband and about her being used to insure his protection and business success resonate with many today. Sarah questions an assumption of patriarchy that the husband's work is more important than the wife's. This assumption has persisted for thousands of years.

The biblical text does not say if Abraham consulted Sarah before taking Isaac to be sacrificed, but Jewish midrash has assumed she was not consulted. Most of the political and economic decision-making in the world is done by males.

Contemporary psychologists and liberation theologians have changed the popular saying, "Power corrupts and absolute power corrupts absolutely," and noted how powerlessness debilitates people. The story has led to discussion that if women do not come forward and offer their perspectives, they may be allowing the possible sacrifice of the future.

# Chapter 4
# Hagar, Used and Abused

## Themes

• Using a person of a different race or class

• Turning against another because of competition

• Deciding whether or not to stay in an abusive situation

• Fearing having a child

• Rejection, anger and confusion

• Fathering a child but not assuming equal responsibility for the welfare of a child

## Possible Uses

• Lenten or reconciliation services

• With single parents, abused spouses or children

• In discussions of racism, refugees, abortion

• With lectionary readings for the twelfth and thirteenth weeks of Ordinary Time, Cycle B

## The Service

(All are seated in a semicircle. At one side are a small stool for the storyteller and a table with a number of candles around a Bible. Leaving the candles unlit during Hagar's sad story and then finally lighting them before the gospel proclamation can be an effective contrast. The tablecloth might be of a rough fabric or of a color related to the storyteller's dress. Since this service uses images of being thrown out into the wilderness, rather than having fresh flowers or greens, some dried branches and/or cactus could be used for an environment. A bowl of salt water, a few bowls if there are a large number present, can be on the table or brought in after the story. Behind the table is hung a batik of a mother hen sheltering her young under her wings based on the mosaic design in a church called "Dominus Flevit," that is, "The Lord Wept" on the Mount of Olives in Jerusalem. The service begins with the music "Sometimes I Feel Like a Motherless Child." (Traditional spiritual, in *Songs of Zion*, ed. J. Jefferson Cleveland [Nashville, TN: Abingdon Press, 1981], softly played to establish a serious mood.)

**First Minister:** Let us pray for open hearts. (Pause) God, in whose image, male and female we are created, so often we have not heard the stories and cries of women. We hear stories of political rulers, military victories, and men of the Bible and the church. Give us ears to hear the cries and stories of your daughters, for your Spirit groans and speaks through them. We pray this in the name of Jesus, who dared to compare himself to a mother hen sheltering her young. Amen. (She gestures for all to be seated.)

(The storyteller, perhaps wearing a loose-fitting dress that is faded or ragged, enters. She has a strength that comes from surviving much pain.)

**Storyteller:** "They call me Hagar, black [or dark] Hagar of Egypt.[1] I am black [or dark] and beautiful,[2] wise, fertile and strong. I was born in the land of Egypt. Our family was poor, and when Abraham, a wealthy nomad who traveled in our country, saw I was young, strong, and promising, he offered my father money to have me as a slave for his wife. I heard Abraham and my father arguing over the price." [The next section should be ironical as she mimics a bargain scene in a market.]

"Abraham has always bargained with both God and people—'Well, if fifty pieces of silver, why not just forty?'[3] My father replied, 'She has good strong legs and good teeth. I am not going to give her away.' But Abraham haggled, 'How about thirty? Are you sure she's worth thirty? I don't see why I should pay any more than twenty.'[4] They finally agreed on thirty." [She gets serious.] "Was I really worth no more than thirty pieces of silver, or is a woman's real worth just never considered?[5] All that matters is that a man can get her for as little as possible. My father could use the money to buy food for my younger sisters and brothers. I was happy about that, but couldn't he have sold me to one of our own country instead of this man who kept wandering farther and farther? This man who said his God was leading him, but he didn't even know where.[6]

Illustration 7: "How Often Have I Longed to Gather You...," by Marha Ann Kirk, CCVI

"I served my mistress, Sarah, as best I could. It was not a bad life. I gathered food, cooked, and helped her cook. I spun, wove, and made clothing. She often spoke to me as a daughter for she was old enough to be my mother." [She stands proudly and slightly gestures to accentuate her firm breasts, then she sags over to show the contrast of Sarah's aging body.] "She saw my breasts grow round and firm. Over the years, hers grew old and sagged, never filling with milk to delight a baby, for her womb was empty. Sometimes I could hear her praying to her God, [she turns her back and looks up and plaintively gestures to a God in the distance] 'Give me a child, O God, You, who promised our descendants would outnumber the grains of sand on the shore, our descendants would be like the stars in the sky, why have you closed my womb? Though my name means beautiful princess, how can Abraham love one who bears him no sons?'

"For years I heard her say the same prayer, then one day she called me. There was hope in her eyes. She said, 'Hagar, you are mine. Through you God shall build a family for me and Abraham. I will tell my husband that you will bear my sons.'"[7] [She sits down looking fearful and confused.] "I don't know how I felt. A woman should always be happy to relate to a man, a woman should always be happy to have a chance to bear children, a woman should always be happy to put her body at the service of another—but I don't know how I felt.[8] I slept with the old Abraham. We had some tender moments." [She doubles her arms over her body as if to shield her vulnerability.] "Yet I wonder, did he do this only to satisfy the wishes of his wife? Did he take me only to have a male descendant? Did I satisfy the lust of an old man? Did he care about me or love me?[9] Was I a person to him or only a beautiful black [or dark] body to play with in the blackness of the night?"[10] [She stands.]

"I conceived a child, and when I knew I trembled in fear. Would my child be a slave or a free person? If I had a daughter, might she too be used by men or sold as my father sold me? When children are sold as slaves among Abraham's people, if it is a son he regains his liberty after six years of service, but a daughter does not."[11] [She holds her stomach.] "Would it be less painful just to get rid of this thing growing within me right now?[12] If I had a son, among slaves would he be resented as of mixed blood, among free people would he be looked down upon? Yet, I had a child in my womb and that was more than my mistress ever had. And I let her know it. Then she began to be cruel to me, though she was the one who gave me to Abraham.

Illustration 8: "Sometimes I feel like a motherless child"

"My mistress abused me, so I fled to the wilderness." [She walks briskly to the far side, but then looks back.] "I found water and I was near the land of Egypt, the land of my people. But in the wilderness I heard a voice. Was it the voice of God or was I foolish and confused? The voice said, 'Go back to your mistress and submit to her abusive treatment. I will make your descendants so numerous that they will be too many to count. Besides, you are now pregnant and shall bear a son; you shall name him Ishmael, For the Lord has heard you, God has answered you. He shall be a wild ass of a man, his hand against everyone, and everyone's hand against him; in opposition to all his kin shall he encamp.' Was this message from my God or was it from the God of Abraham and Sarah? The voice said, 'Go back to your mistress and submit to her abusive treatment.' Would my God turn my eyes from my own land or my feet from freedom and tell me to go back to bondage and abuse? I returned, but I still wonder if that was the voice of my God or their God.[13]

"Anyway, I bore a son, a beautiful black [or dark] son looking like me, and Abraham called him Ishmael." [She gestures as if cradling and kissing a baby. The next part should invite humor.] "He was the cutest baby you have ever seen—you think all mothers say that? But he really was. He was the delight of his father's heart. At first my mistress claimed him as her own. I cared for him, but dared not comment as she said to others, 'Look at my child.' But all of that changed when she conceived." [This should invite humor.] "Can you believe this—she was ninety years old and she got pregnant. You laugh? She did, too. In fact, that is his name—Isaac, laughter. What a joke that this could happen. Young Ishmael was fascinated by the new baby and loved his little brother.

"But my mistress's heart hardened toward my child. She began to refer to Ishmael as the 'child of the slave' and to Isaac as 'my child.' On the day Isaac was weaned, Abraham gave a great party." [She mimics an evil look and whisper.] "My mistress watched Ishmael play with Isaac, and then I heard her say to the old man who had fathered them both, 'Drive out that slave and her son! No son of that slave is going to share the inheritance with my son Isaac!'"

[This is said slowly with disbelief and horror.] "Is this why the God of Abraham and Sarah brought me back from the wilderness? To give birth to a child to be claimed by another, then to be rejected? For me to be abused by the woman I served as one might serve a mother? To be thrown out by the man to whom I gave my body? To see my precious son loved and then ignored? To see my son the heir thrown out? And I, am

I good enough to be used, but never to be respected? Use my body then toss it out?" [She turns away almost in tears, then turns back with the quiet strength of mothers through the ages who have made it on their own.]

"Early the next morning Abraham came to our tent. The man who fathered this child put bread and water in my hand and the child on my back, but he would not look into my eyes. He sent us out into the wilderness of Beer-sheba, a wilderness where people die." [She imitates the movements spoken of in the next section.] "It was hot. I walked and walked. When there was no more water than my tears, I put the child down under a bush and I turned the other way because I did not want to watch him as he died. A mother should not have to watch her own child die. Then Ishmael cried, and a God who didn't seem to listen to a mother's cries heard the cries of a boy, and I opened my eyes. There was a well of water. I filled the skin with water and let my child drink. He grew up and lived in the wilderness of Paran. I found my son a wife from my country, Egypt. They have children. Yet, people do not call them my children as that voice in the wilderness had promised; they call them Abraham's children.[14] And still the children of Isaac look down on my children.

"I search for a black [or dark] God of black [or dark] children. I search for a mother God to hear my motherly cries.[15] I search for a sister God to teach Sarah and me to be sisters not rivals.[16] I am despised and rejected, the outcast of men.[17] Is there any God who cares for Hagar?" [She goes and stands facing the wall, reaching up in anguish. After a few seconds of silence, she begins to dance "Sometimes I Feel Like a Motherless Child," which is sung by one person. The dance should be heavy, grounded, and strong. She ends staring in the distance and walking away. There is some silence. People may be invited to write a dialogue with Hagar, or the service may continue.]

**Second Minister:** We have heard the story of a person confused and rejected we have heard the cries of one treated unjustly. The prophets cried and acted out their laments. Do we dare listen to the cries? Those who do not open their hearts to feel the pain, do not have room to receive the grace. Now, let us close our eyes and listen to cries from around the world. After each thought, let us join in prayer by expressing a groan or a sigh.

(Groaning prayer can be a very powerful experience, but the ministers may need to model the response the first few times for people to get in the mood for it. While people are praying the litany with closed eyes, someone may light the candles.)

**Third Minister:** One hundred and thirty million more females than males do not have opportunities to learn to read; [Groan in response after each of these.]

• Though women may vote in most countries, women hold less than ten percent of the seats in legislatures, and in the Third World, less than seven percent;

• In the United States, women hold less than fifteen percent of elected offices;

• Hardly anywhere do laws actually give women and children rights and protection equal to men's;

• Two-thirds of the women and half of the men over twenty-five in developing countries have not been to school;

• In no part of the world are there curriculums which equally value the childbearing, caregiving, work, history, or writings of women;

• No major religion of the world challenges such prejudice against females;

• Women produce at least forty percent of the world's food, but only own about one percent of the world's land, and thus lack legal protection and benefits;

• Women are the sole supporters of one-fourth to one-third of all the families in the world;

• Fifty percent of black families in the United States are headed by women;

• In this country, seventy-five percent of the poor are women and children;

• Within three years after a divorce, only nineteen percent of the fathers continue to pay child support;

• Women earn on an average sixty-four cents to every dollar a man makes, but it is lower for black, Hispanic, and Asian women;

• In the United States, every one to three minutes another woman is beaten within her home;

• Every two to five minutes another woman is raped;

• Every five to ten minutes another little girl is molested by her father;

• For every white woman raped, there are twelve black women raped;

• In countries torn by military violence, there is even more rape than in the United States;

Statistics represent "people with the tears wiped away."[18]

(Then the people may be invited to pray aloud or in the depths of their hearts for those persons or situations which are in need.)

**First:** From the beginning until now, the entire creation has been groaning in one great act of giving birth; and not only creation, but all of us who possess the first fruits of the Spirit, we too groan inwardly as we wait for our bodies to be set free [Rom. 8:22, JB]. We join our groans, our cries, our prayers with the motherly Spirit who knows how to pray through us our needs too deep for words. Amen.

**Second:** Now let us open our eyes, our ears, and our hearts to the words of the gospel.

(She walks over to the Bible on the table. She gestures for all to stand, holds up the Bible and then opens it, and very slowly reads part of one verse.)

**Second:** Jesus said, "Jerusalem, Jerusalem, you that kill the prophets and stone those who are sent to you! How often have I longed to gather your children, as a hen gathers her brood under her wings." [Luke 13:34, JB]. This is the good news. (She closes the Bible, holds it up, then places it back on the table.)

**Third:** Hagar wandered in the desert without water, without consolation, without knowledge of a God like her, a mother God who understood or cared. Like Jesus who looked at the city of Jerusalem, like Jesus who loved Lazarus, Hagar wept. Let us remember their tears Let us remember the tears of the suffering throughout the world. May we weep with those who weep. May this ocean of tears become an ocean of new life—water of our tears, water of the womb, water of a new birth in which there is no longer Jew or Gentile, slave or free, male or female. Let us come forward and anoint each other with this salt water as tears.

(The three ministers anoint each others' cheeks with tears and then gesture for the participants to come and do the same. As this is going on, Colleen Fulmer's

"Rest in My Wings," found in the Appendix, is sung. The chant, "Gentle loving God, the mother of my soul, hold me as your own," by Rufino Zaragoza, O.F.M. Conv. [*National Catholic Reporter*, P. O. Box 281, Kansas City, MO 64141], might also be used.)

**First:** (She gestures for people to stand.) Let us pray in gratitude and hope. (Pause) God, not only of Abraham and Sarah, God of Hagar, you hear the groans and cries of the weak ones throughout the world. May the stories and tears we have experienced today give us courage to unite and create a world of healing and compassion. May we feel Christ who like a mother bird shelters us, and may we learn to shelter others with such tender love. This we pray in His name. Amen.

(This service can end quietly or it can end with "We Are the Body of Christ, by Martha Ann Kirk and Colleen Fulmer which is found in the Appendix.)

**First:** The second-century text, the Acts of John, speaks of Jesus and the disciples doing a circle dance at the Last Supper. The text probably reflects the early Christians, practice of dancing when they gathered for Eucharist. Join in this circle dance, praying that we may be more and more transformed into the Body of Christ. We are one in our weeping, but we are also one in our healing and dancing. Gather in a circle, follow my gestures on the chorus and walk to the right on the verses.

# For Further Reflection, Journalizing, and/or Discussion

Scriptural Background: Genesis 16 and 21

### Questions

1. Abraham bargains with God for Sodom and Gomorrah as a trader would bargain in a marketplace (Gen. 19:22-33). Though scripture does not record how Abraham got Hagar, in this story Abraham bargains to get her for as little as possible. How do we convey to people that they are worth very little?

2. Have you ever found it difficult to define your real feelings and needs because society has defined certain roles you should fulfill and in which you should be happy?

3. How have we described God as the God of a higher race, class, or sex?

4. Hagar's story was written by owners of slaves rather than by slaves. It was written by the Hebrews, the descendants of Sarah and Abraham. Might the Arabs, the descendants of Hagar and Abraham, tell the story differently? How do each of us tell stories from our own perspectives? What is the "true" perspective?

5. Have you ever turned against a friend when you have found yourself in a difficult or oppressive situation?

6. Many of the women in scripture are remembered because they were mothers or ancestors of famous men. How can women learn that they have value in themselves, not just in being spouses or parents? How can men learn that they have equal responsibility for parenting? How can parenting be kept in perspective as not the only activity or value of mothers or fathers?

7. Oppressed peoples often internalize the message of their oppressors and think of themselves as inferior or to blame for the oppression. Is it God's will that persons stay in or go back to situations that demean them as human beings or situations in which they experience psychological or physical abuse?

8. How can we each discern which relationships are relationships of mutual respect to which we should be faithful though it may be difficult? How can we discern which relationships are oppressive? How can Jesus, who came to "proclaim liberty to captives, recovery of sight to the blind and release to prisoners" (Luke 4:18) help persons break out of oppressive relationships?

9. Hagar cries out seeking a God like a sister to teach her and Sarah to live as sisters and not as rivals. Do we have sisters or women friends who have helped us know a "Sister God?" Do we know a "Sister God" who has helped us value women?

### Readings

• Women listed as property (Exod. 20:17)

• Daughters sold as slaves not gaining freedom as men (Exod. 21:7)

• Men had rights to have many wives and to divorce when they wished (Deut. 21:10 and 24:1)

• "The Emergence of Black Feminist Consciousness," by Katie Geneva Cannon, and "Every Two Minutes: Battered Women and Feminist Interpretation," by Susan Brooks Thistlethwaite, in *Feminist Interpretation of the Bible*, edited by Letty M. Russell.

## Reflections on the Development and Use of the Service

This story, like that of Miriam and Susana, has been hard for me to perform because I have been conditioned as a woman not to express angry or negative feelings, but rather to "accept the cross and offer it up." While I have had ability to preach and lead prayers on a nurturing and tender God, I have not had skills to express publicly prophetic strength or challenges. Literature including scripture has so often portrayed strong women as evil women. This story of Hagar has often received extreme praise or blame. A black woman seminarian said that it was one of the most meaningful worship experiences she has had. Another black woman suggested that Hagar be identified as "dark" rather than "black," thus inviting the identification of more people with her.

When the story was shared in a Catholic Sunday Eucharist, a few seminarians said that it was not a good liturgy because "Hagar sounded angry." The priest who presided felt that such a story needed to be told. The same service prompted a number of women to say that it was an extremely meaningful experience for them. They as women had sometimes felt "used as slaves" but thrown out when it came to respect or opportunity. They had never before heard a homily which dealt with their pain. A mother who had given her children away for adoption found the story, as used at a women's conference, an opportunity to talk about and work through her twenty years of unresolved grief.

Women's dialogues about the story contributed to its development. Their discussions of fears of having a child and considerations of abortion led to mentioning these. Another woman's comments about the ambiguity of feelings in having sexual intercourse led to Hagar's comments that she had "some tender moments" with Abraham, but all the while wondered if he loved or was using her. A friend's story of being raped and having a child of mixed racial identity led to that issue. The sad stories of a number of friends going through divorces, and my own experience of being "alone in the wilderness" to do prayer from women's perspectives unsupported by traditional patriarchal scholarship are interwoven in Hagar's story and the prayers. The story received very favorable response in a seminar on "Women in Transition" at the National Presbyterian Women's Meeting and seems particularly appropriate in programs dealing with that issue.

# Chapter 5

# Miriam the Prophetess Led Them in Praise

## Themes

• Civil disobedience to a political system which does not protect innocent lives

• Cooperation with others of different ethnic groups and social classes to preserve life

• Claiming one's God-given freedom and leading others in the same direction

• Leading worship to praise and thank God

• Leading dance to claim the joy and freedom God gives

• Continuing to search for a promised land of freedom and justice

## Possible Uses

• Passover or Holy Saturday

• With lectionary readings of the fifteenth week of Ordinary Time, Cycle A

• Peace programs, child-protection programs, expressions of solidarity with oppressed peoples

## The Service

(The chairs are arranged in circle or semicircle. A small table with a cloth that relates to the color of the storyteller's dress has a Bible, one or more containers of oil, candles, and some flowers or branches. If it is possible to get them, many percussion instruments such as tambourines, bells, triangles, claves, finger cymbals, timbrels, and maracas, as well as streamers or ribbons, will make Miriam's dance more festive. Before the service begins, the storyteller explains that singing, playing, and dancing are ways of claiming the freedom that God gives us. Within the service, she will invite the participants to do this. She gives out the instruments and ribbons. She invites them to practice by standing, clapping, and singing "Miriam's Song," by Colleen Fulmer, which may be found in the Appendix. When this introduction has been done with humor and enthusiasm, almost always some of the people have joyfully joined in dancing around with Miriam in the story, and all the rest have helped clap and sing. Also, a few people might be prepared to come forth and do a circle dance around Miriam.)

**First Minister:** The opposite of love of God is not hate, but fear. Do you have any fears that hold you back from whole heartedly responding to God's call and plans for you? (This should be done humorously.) Stand up and reach into your heart and take out those fears and throw them away. Take them out and throw them up. Take them out and throw them down. As we sing the song, "Choose Life," we are going to throw the fears away during the verses. (This song by Colleen Fulmer may be found in the Appendix.) As we sing the chorus, "Choose life that you might live, choose peace that you might see a tomorrow. Let justice roll, roll like a river, flow like a river down," walk around the room snapping your fingers and telling everybody this. Also, tell our leaders, tell the Russians, tell the Pentagon, tell the people in the Middle East....Let us join with the courageous women whose stories we shall hear. They risked their own lives to preserve life.

("Choose Life" is sung. There is enough time for people to return to their places. It is desirable to have printed programs that have the comments about women prophets and the texts of the responses in word and song.)

**Second Minister:** Before I formed you in the womb I knew you; before you were born I dedicated you; a prophetess to the nations I appointed you.

**All:** O Loving God, I know not how to speak; I am a woman.

**Second:** Do not say, "I am a woman." To whomever I send you, you shall go; whatever I command you, you shall speak. Have no fear, for I am with you to deliver you. You shall root up and tear down, destroy and demolish, but you shall also build and plant [adapted from Jer. 1].

**First:** While the Judeo-Christian tradition has preserved eighteen books of the activities, sermons and saying of the prophets, only four prophetesses of God are mentioned by name—Miriam, Deborah, Huldah, and Anna—and little of their stories is given. Let us claim their stories; let us claim the stories of prophetesses through the ages; let us claim our own stories. (She gestures for all to be seated.)

(The storyteller, perhaps in a loose, bright-colored dress, comes forward, looks around establishing eye contact with the people, and begins with prophetic strength and intensity.)

**Storyteller:** "Choose life, I say to you, choose life, that you and your descendants may live and flourish in the land our God has given to all the human family. Choose life, though you must risk your own life to bring to birth, to nurture, and to preserve life in the face of the forces of death.

"I am the Hebrew prophetess born in the land of Egypt, the first Hebrew prophetess called by name. I am the daughter of Sarah, woman of faith who went to a strange land trusting the God who leads us to unknown places. I am the daughter of Rachel and Rebecca, who gave their flesh and blood that the family of God might be carried on. I am the daughter of Jochebed, a daughter of Levi whose family was to lead the worship of Yahweh."[1]

(She makes a joyful broad gesture as if leading a huge congregation, then suddenly her mood changes. She hunches over and crosses her arms as if they were bound and continues with anguish, but finally defiant strength.)

"I am the daughter of generations and generations of slave women in bondage. We are beaten in our bondage but we grow strong in our pain. I am Miriam, the prophetess.

"The Egyptian pharaoh, as hundreds of wars and political systems before him and thousands of wars and political systems after him, would destroy our nation by destroying our men. He does not think the women matter.[2] The life of a nation is not only in its men." [This is done to invite humor mimicking the great pharaoh and the lowly midwives who cleverly outwit him.] "The pharaoh called our midwives, Puah and Shiphrah, and said 'When you act as midwives for the Hebrew women and see them giving birth, if it is a boy, kill him; but if it is a girl, she may live.'"[3]

(She speaks with compassion.) "Could these midwives—daughters of Yahweh, the rock who bore us, the compassionate one who writhed in labor pains to give us life—could these daughters of Sarah, Rebecca, and Rachel who struggled to give birth, destroy a child as it first saw the light of day?[4] Puah and Shiphrah, ushers into the land of the living, put the laws of God before the laws of man." [She continues with humor.] "Then, the mighty pharaoh noticed that the nation was growing and he called those midwives back. He asked, 'How is it that the Hebrews are multiplying?' [She quakes with fear, but then with a wink at the people continues.] "The midwives said, 'The Hebrew women are not like the Egyptian women. They are robust and give birth before the midwife arrives.' Yes, we women are strong, but we need each other in our birthings and our nurturing, we need each other to preserve life.[5]

"When my brother Moses was born, our mother, Jochebed, feared for his life. Would the systems of death stalk this baby as he grew? She put him in a papyrus basket that would float, and hid him in the reeds near the edge of the Nile. I stood guard nearby. The sun was brilliant and touched the multicolored dress of the lovely young woman who came to the edge of the river to delight in its cool waters. I knew the woman was of the royal family. She smiled, laughed, and talked with those who seemed to be her maids. Their chatter was pierced by the cry of the baby awakened by them. I trembled. Will these Egyptian women know that this boy wrapped in the swaddling clothes of the poor is a Hebrew? Will they consider his life a threat to their power and have the child killed? I tiptoed near to listen." [She acts out taking, holding, and comforting a baby.] "They followed the cries and opened the basket. The woman looked at his tiny hands and red, tear-streaked face. She was moved with pity for him and said, 'It is one of the Hebrews' children.' She picked him up, held him close to her heart, and rocked him. All eyes were on this fragile one who cried out for life. She was an Egyptian. He was a Hebrew boy, and she knew it. She was a princess, and he was of a despised group of slaves who threatened the power system.

"Moses cried again and I could stand it no longer. I left my hiding place and went straight up to the woman. 'Shall I go and call one of the Hebrew women to nurse the child for you?' I asked. Her dark eyes looked over my ragged dress, my bare dirty feet and finally into my face, clearly the face of a Hebrew. I felt bold and strong like the midwives. She must have felt compassionate like the midwives. 'Yes,' she said, 'Can you get someone to nurse the child?' She looked again at his soft face, 'Can you get someone to nurse my child?' I gently took him from her arms, our eyes met, both knowing what neither of us dared say."[6] [She takes the baby and starts to laugh.] "Do you know Mother got paid for nursing her own baby!

"Moses grew strong on his own mother's milk. He grew wise as he heard our women's stories of the God who loves us with an everlasting love and who wishes freedom and dignity for all. Moses grew rich in knowledge as he lived in the palace of his second mother, the princess. He learned what it is like to be a free person, he learned of laws, he learned of governing people."

[She acts out an overseer whipping a slave.] "One day, he saw a Hebrew slave brutally struck by an Egyptian. Though he never spoke of our people, of the mother who nursed him and of me who cared for him, his heart was with us and he killed the Egyptian and buried him in the sand." [She gestures indicating this and then fleeing.] "He had to flee for his life to the land of Midian. I wondered if I would ever see him again.

"Forty years passed and our bondage grew worse; Hebrew life was cheap. Though the midwives preserved life, was life as a slave worth living? Is it life to be little more than an ox or an ass?" [She turns and raises her hands pleading with a God far away.] "I cried out to God, 'You created us male and female in your image. Why do you leave us in this misery?' Our God heard our groaning. Moses with hair and beard grown long, Moses with wisdom and strength refined in shepherd's wandering, returned. He and our brother, Aaron, spoke of God who wished freedom for all the daughters and sons of Sarah and Abraham. I had spoken to the women of this for years, and now was the time for me to let the women know that our God was going to free us. We are destined for a land where children live, a land where we stand free and tall, imaging the God who bore us, imaging in our compassion, in our strength, in our ability to share our milk of sustenance and our milk of wisdom.

"Yet, the pharaoh was not ready to give us our freedom—that never happens. One has to take freedom. God was on our side. When pharaoh and all the Egyptians knew suffering, when they knew what it was like for children to be killed, we finally had the chance to escape from their grasp. Moses, Aaron, and I led the people out of the land of bondage."[7] [She excitedly indicates how the sea moved and how they marched through.] "Our God made the sea open, the waters leapt up before us, the dry land supported our joyful feet. And when we arrived on the other shore. I knew myself as a woman, strong and beautiful, preserving life as our God, freed from bondage and freeing others. We glorify God in our bodies; we claim the freedom our God has given in our bodies. Like hundreds of prophetesses before me filled with the spirit of God, like thousands of prophetesses after me filled with the spirit of God, I led the people in prayer."

Illustration 9: Miriam took a tambourine and led the people in praise

Illustration 10: Our God wants freedom for all

(As she picks up a tambourine, "Miriam's Song," by Colleen Fulmer, which can be found in the Appendix, begins. Large gestures with a tambourine with lots of ribbons tied on it can make this festive. At first, the music is soft as she speaks, but then it builds as they dance.)

"I led the people in praise. I picked up a tambourine and led the people in dance.[8] Yahweh our God has done wonderful things. We claim the freedom God has given by dancing and praising God. If you have been freed from bondage, join in the dance." [She looks at different people in the audience and gestures for all to rise and join in singing and dancing as she speaks.] "If you have ever been freed from fear or from doubt, join in the dance. If you have ever been freed from selfishness, from indifference; if you have ever been freed by our God, will you join in the dance? Sisters and brothers, let us praise God for our freedom. Will you join in the dance?"

(The refrain might be sung many times as they sing and dance. Finally, she puts down the tambourine and leads them getting slower and softer. She gestures for them to be seated. She might improvise, "I can see that you are people God has freed....You know what is means to come from bondage...." then she continues the story.)

"We danced and danced all the night. Our God is a God of freedom, of dance, of life. A God who gives us laws that we may choose life. Moses received the laws and we journeyed on through the desert. In the desert, our God cared for us as a mother cares for her children, providing food and water, seeing that our clothes did not wear out.[9] Our God carried us as a mother carries a child."[10] [She walks away as if tenderly carrying a child, then turns back around looking tired and weary.]

"It's a long, long way to the promised land. We've wandered over three decades in this desert. Sometimes I think we are near our God in the desert, and other times it seems to completely separate us from God. In our pain and frustration Aaron and I spoke against Moses." [She begins to look at her hands and arms and gasps at the sight of leprosy.] "I was punished with leprosy, but Aaron was not. Am I destined for suffering because I am a woman? Can a man go free while a woman is condemned? Why are things different for men and women?[11] In the depths of my heart I have wondered if Moses feared me or was jealous of me that day after crossing the Red Sea when I led prayer and dance. Our God had freed me, and I could do no less than claim that strength and freedom. The priestesses of Egypt lead their people in worship. Should our God receive less praise, less service?[12] Anyway, I was put outside the camp with leprosy, but the people would not travel on without me." [She wipes her hands across her face and her arms as if indicating leprosy being washed off.] "For seven days I suffered, but then Moses prayed for me and God cured me and we continued our journey."

(She walks away, with her back turned puts on a shawl over her head, and then returns as a stooped, weary, old woman. Soft, melancholy music can intensify the mood of this last section.)

"Yes, for over three decades we have journeyed in this wilderness. I am old now and I am tired. Will I reach the land our God has promised? Will we ever reach the land where the lives of the poor are as precious as those of the rich? Will we ever reach the land where daughters are considered as valuable as sons and daughters' names are remembered? The land where the lives of children are prized more than the systems of power, prestige, and wealth? Will we ever reach the land where our daughters can lead the assembly in praise or the nation in making laws for peace and justice?[13] A land where freed people join in the dance, celebrating their bodies as temples of God? A promised land where Egyptian and Hebrew, young and old, dance together? I am old. I will die soon. Will *you* reach the promised land?"

(She slowly and intensely looks at the people, then walks away. Soft music continues for a while.)

**Second:** (She takes the bible from the table, gestures for all to rise, and slowly reads.) A reading from the holy gospel according to Mark.

"When Jesus was in Bethany reclining at table in the house of Simon the leper, a woman entered carrying an alabaster jar of perfume made from expensive aromatic nard. Breaking the jar, she began to pour the perfume on his head....Wherever the good news is proclaimed throughout the world, what she has done will be told in her memory."

This is the good news [Mark 14:3 and 9, NAB].

**First:** Wherever the good news is proclaimed this story will be told *in memory of her*—and yet the story does not even give her name. Also, this story seems to be confused with other stories, and none of her words are recorded. Why do we not have the words and the visions of Miriam, the prophetess, as we have those of Amos, Ezekiel, Jeremiah and Isaiah? Why do we not have the name and words of this woman who anointed the head of Jesus? Wise persons who could recognize leaders and prophets anointed them with oil to give them strength and courage for their missions. As Elisabeth Schussler Fiorenza notes, this woman could recognize Jesus and anoint him for his ministry, a ministry of service, a ministry of suffering. This woman could anoint Him to see visions and to speak the truth. She recognized what the men seemed to miss.[14] Can we recognize what the ministry of the Christ is meant to be? (Pause)

(The ministers hold up the oil.)

**Second:** Let us stretch forth our hands and bless this oil. Loving God, who strengthened the midwives to obey your laws of life rather than a man's laws of death, who brought your people from bondage to freedom;

**First:** Who delighted in a ritual of praise and dance led by your prophetess Miriam, who called women through the ages to prophesy, who led a woman to anoint Jesus for his ministry of service and suffering;

**Second:** Bless this oil and bless us as we anoint each other to share in his ministry. (Pause for silent prayer.)

**First:** Let us be generous anointing head or hands or heart....we need much healing and strength on this journey. (The ministers anoint each other and gesture for others to come do the same. As this is going on, there is soft instrumental music.)

**Second:** God of strength and compassion, through the ages you have filled women with your Ruah, your Spirit, to prophesy. We praise you as we celebrate the companions you have sent to lead us on the way to the promised land.

(A cantor sings the response, "Send us strength, be our sisters," and all repeat this. The music, by Colleen Fulmer, may be found in the Appendix. As the litany is said, there is soft strumming, and after each group of petitions, the response is sung.)

**First:**

• Deborah, prophetess and leader who stood up when men were afraid;

• Huldah, prophetess who warned the nation that their unfaithfulness would bring suffering;

• Ruth and Naomi, who supported and cared for each other;

• Esther and Judith, who risked their lives to save their people;

• Mary, who spoke of the mighty being put down from their thrones and the lowly being raised up; [Response]

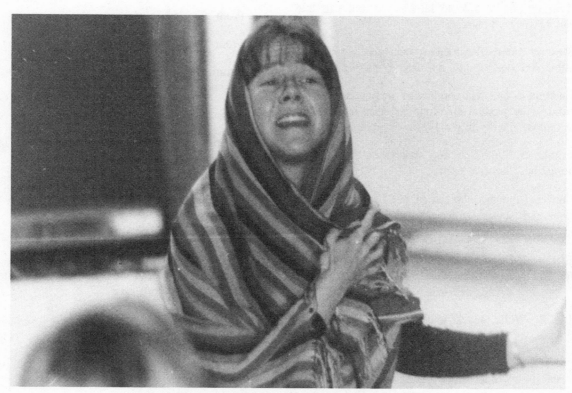

Illustration 11: Will we ever reach the promised land?

• Mary Magdalene, who was sent as the apostle to the apostles;

• Priscilla, Lydia, Chloe, Phoebe, Nympha, Junia, Mary, and others who spread the good news and led the community in prayer;

• Sts. Agnes, Cecilia, Perpetua and Felicitas who were martyred for keeping faith in the Resurrected One;

• St. Claire of Assisi, who persevered in her dream for her community's lifestyle despite the opposition of Rome for twenty years;

• St. Catherine of Siena, who challenged kings, cardinals, and popes to give up corruption and live the gospels; [Response]

• St. Teresa of Avila, who called the Spanish church to reform, though rejected by the pope's delegate who said the "voice of a woman should not be heard in the church";

• Sts. Angela Merici, Louise de Marillac, and Jane Frances de Chantal, who courageously worked for active ministry for women when religious women were to be confined to cloisters;

• Sor Juana Inez de la Cruz, who was one of the most brilliant people of colonial Mexico, but was told by the clergy to give up studies;

• Blessed Kateri Tekakwitha, who was rejected by her Native American family and friends for her faith;

• Lucretia Mott, who organized demonstrations of black and white women marching together in Philadelphia to oppose slavery in the 1830s; [Response]

• Sojourner Truth, former slave who became an abolitionist and feminist orator;

• Harriet Tubman, who risked her life to lead over three hundred slaves to freedom through the underground railroad;

• Elizabeth Cady Stanton and Susan B. Anthony, who for fifty years worked with the women's movement until it became a national force;

• Ida B. Wells, black journalist who dared write about and expose the brutal lynchings of blacks by white mobs;

• Anne Frank and Edith Stein, who did not lose faith and hope in God though six million Jews around them were exterminated while most Christians kept silence; [Response]

• Dorothy Day, who consistently supported nonviolence and helped the poor through founding Catholic Worker Houses;

• Rosa Parks, black woman who sat in the white section of a segregated bus in 1955;

• Maura Clark, Jean Donovan, Ita Ford, Dorothy Kazel, and many others who have been slain for resisting oppression in Latin America;

• Filomena Asuncion, a Philippina Methodist deaconess, who was killed for gathering and teaching the poor to claim their human rights;

• Nameless women throughout the world who have spoken and lived the prophetic word burning deep in their hearts. [Response]

(The cantor sings, "Set us free, God our sister," and all repeat. Again there is strumming and the response after each group of petitions.)

**Second:**

• From timidity,

• From narrowness, bitterness, and pettiness,

• From blindness, coldness, insensitivity,

• From clinging to old securities,

• From lack of imagination,

• From thinking we must save the world when Jesus already has.

[Response]

• From seeking our own freedom while ignoring other's bondage,

• From seriousness and sourness when laughter is your gift,

• From saying we are weak when you have given us strength enough,

• From living in our heads when you relate to us through our whole bodies,

• From accepting other people's responsibilities when they need to learn to bear them,

• From blaming ourselves when we have been the victims of others.

[Response]

• From denying our experience and inner wisdom,

• From manipulation and dishonesty,

• From jealousy and competition,

• From denying and hiding our gifts,

• From refusing to accept power when it could be used to empower many,

• From keeping silence when you have put your words in our hearts and on our lips.

[Response]

**First:** God, powerful and compassionate, today fill us with your Spirit, to follow the example of your prophetesses through the ages. This we pray in the name of Jesus, our brother and our friend. Amen.

### First Option

**Storyteller:** Let us gather in a circle and sing and dance, "Ruah;" follow my gestures on the chorus and dance to the right on the verses. (This song, by Colleen Fulmer, and the movements can be found in the Appendix.)

### Second Option

**Storyteller:** We now have the technical ability to get a bomb anyplace in the world in two minutes. Yet in thousands of places throughout the world, families do not have water in their homes. Women often spend hours carrying water. We have remembered the God of the Exodus who saw that her children had water, food, and clothes. Let us celebrate that God. Follow my gestures on the chorus and sing this song as you learn it.

("Washerwoman God" by Martha Ann Kirk and Colleen Fulmer which is found in the Appendix is sung and danced.)

## For Further Reflection, Journalizing, and/or Discussion

Scriptural Background: Exod. 1, 2, and 15:20-21; Num. 12:1-15 and 20:1; Deut. 24:9; Micah 6:4.

### Questions

1. What are your hopes and dreams for a promised land?

2. What do we need along the way to the promised land? How can we sustain one another on the journey?

3. When oppressed people are freed, they often do not know what to do with freedom. Is it possible to find security by returning to bondage?

4. How can women of different ages, classes, and nations cooperate to save life today?

5. The God who freed the Hebrews from Egyptian slavery is often depicted as a male warrior; the God who sustained them in the wilderness is sometimes depicted doing women's work, providing for a family as a mother might. The Hebrew word for womb, *rechem*, is used in the plural to mean mercy, compassion, *rachamin* (e.g., Jer. 31:20). Do we ever expect mothers to care for children more faithfully than fathers? Is this an insult to father's capabilities? Is it fair to mothers?

6. God does what were considered women's tasks—providing food, water, clothing (Neh. 9:20b-21). If women have opportunities to do what was once considered "men's work," why is it important that men be freed to do "women's work"?

7. Women have participated in many liberation movements (the Exodus, the French and American revolutions, and the Marxist revolution). Why have none of these brought a promised land in which women have the respect, opportunities, or freedom that men have?

8. Biblical women's stories often celebrate a reversal of the social order: God's surprising intervention on behalf of the weak. (See "Readings," below.) What can the weakest in our world (children, the handicapped, the retarded, the poor, and the powerless) teach us?

9. Women often have a strong sense of bodiliness, perhaps related to their capacity to give birth, and use dance to relate to God as Miriam did. How can bodily involvement (eating, different postures, anointing, dance, washing, processions, the kiss of peace, yoga, gestures, laying on of hands) help us more deeply enter into prayer?

10. The prophets sometimes have moments of intense religious feeling which help to sustain them. Have you ever known moments of intense religious feeling like that which Miriam knew when she led the dance? Have these feelings led you to be stronger, more loving and generous?

11. How can we learn to encourage each other's gifts of leadership rather than be jealous or threatened by them?

## Readings

• Praising God through dance (S of S 7; Ps. 45; Jdt. 15:13; II Sam. 6:14; Exod. 15:20; Ps. 150)

Women sing of liberation:

• Miriam (Exod. 15:21)

• Deborah (Judg. 5:1-31)

• Judith (Jdt. 16:1-20)

• Hannah (I Sam. 2:1-10)

• Mary (Luke 1:46-55)

Other prophetesses:

• Deborah (Judg. 4-5)

• Huldah (II Kgs 22:14-20)

• Anna (Luke 2:36-38)

# Reflections on the Devolpment and Use of the Service

The story of Miriam has been used both with this anointing ritual and with a ritual of bread and water, recalling the manna and water to sustain the people in the wilderness, as well as in Eucharists or Communion services.

The story is appropriate in many contexts of prayers and programs for peace and justice. The story involves inviting the audience to rise and participate in singing, clapping, and dancing. This dynamic of audience movement has been very effective in involving people with the story. Though an occasional person has mentioned being uncomfortable, there have been large numbers of people enthusiastic about the movement. This leads me to believe that we do not give our congregations enough invitations for participative movement. How do we empower them for prophetic action if we suppress their feelings and movements within worship? Doug Adams writes, "Much of David's success in building the consciousness of community in early Israel and unifying the tribes is attributed to his ability in leading others in dance and communal celebration."[15] Miriam the dance leader, like David the dance leader, could have had great influence in the community through this skill. My own experience has been that dance leadership in worship significantly unites and energizes the people. When the leader of the dance is not ordained, hierarchical power is threatened. Dance empowers all who participate. It redistributes power.[16] Adams has written on Miriam's dance as one of joy and on the ability of dance to liberate people. He notes that, "the dance at the Exodus is most appropriate as a watershed between slavery and freedom, the past and the future."[17] In the responses from people who have participated in this service, the Miriam dance has been a watershed between hierarchical power in worship and mutual empowerment.

# Chapter 6

# Ruth And Naomi, Companions in the Bitterness and Sweetness of Life

## Themes

• Supporting other women

• Caring for the elderly

• Accepting a person of another race or group

• Carrying on after a loved one dies

• Taking initiative and being resourceful in a difficult situation

• Calling others to fulfillment of their duty in justice and charity

## Possible Uses

• With lectionary readings for the twentieth week of Ordinary Time, Cycle I; with *An Inclusive Language Lectionary,* alternative reading for the twelfth Sunday of Pentecost, Cycle B

• With widows

• Intergenerational programs, women's retreats, programs on friendship, racism

## The Service

(The chairs should be arranged in a semicircle with a table in the opening and a small stool. The table should be covered with a cloth in colors relating to the storyteller's dress and have an oil lamp like the ones used in biblical times, or a candle. If the second option at the end of the service is used, then a Bible is needed on the table. The storyteller enters with a basket of fruit, with a sour fruit such as a lemon or lime and a sweet fruit such as an apple or peach on top. She places the basket on the table.)

**First Minister:** The Hebrew word for Spirit is *ruah,* a feminine word meaning air or breath. The image in the first chapter of Genesis, "The Spirit of God hovered over the waters," is that of a mother bird hovering over her young, sheltering them. This Spirit of God gathers us together, from across the country, from around the world. Let us gather in a circle—women, men, old ones, young ones, aliens, relatives—learning from each other's wisdom and stories, dancing as one people. Sing and follow my gestures on the chorus and circle to the right on the verses. (Some of the verses, including the eighth about Ruth, are sung from "Ruah," by Colleen Fulmer. The song and movements may be found in the Appendix.)

**Second Minister:** Let us bow our heads and pray. (Pause) Gracious God, El Shaddai, open our hearts to hear the ancient story of women who cared for each other in the bitterness and sweetness of life. Open our hearts to hear our own deep stories of the bitterness and the sweetness of our own lives, and to realize that you are with us through it all. This we pray in the name of Jesus, the great storyteller who lives and reigns with you forever and ever. Amen. (She gestures for every one to be seated.)

(When people are seated, the first verse and chorus of "El Shaddai" by Colleen Fulmer, which can be found in the Appendix, is softly played or sung by one person. Printed programs could have this note about the imagery of the song: "El Shaddai," a Hebrew name, means 'God of the high places.' The name also means "the God who has breasts." *Shad* is the Hebrew word for 'breast.' *El* means 'God.' Perhaps the shape of mountain peaks suggested this dual meaning. God has been compared to a mother who "tenderly holds the one she loves against her breasts." There is soft strumming as the storyteller enters with the basket of fruit. She places it on the table, and holds up and looks at a lemon or other sour fruit and an apple or other sweet fruit. Then, she sits thoughtfully. As the music fades, she rises and begins speaking.)

**Storyteller:** "I call myself Ruth, the daughter of Naomi.[1] Oh, others may call me 'that Moabite woman, that foreigner' or the widow of Mahlon, or now the wife of Boaz or the mother of Obed—but I call myself the daughter of Naomi, Ruth the daughter, in fact, even the friend, of Naomi. Precious old Naomi has gone through sweetness and bitterness, sweetness and bitterness."2 [She holds up the apple as the says, "sweet-ness" and the lemon as she says, "bitterness."] She and Elimelech married, were blessed with two sons, Mahlon and Chilion, but there was a famine in Bethlehem so they came to the fertile plains of Moab, my country. For a time Naomi knew some sweetness, but then her husband died. Eventually her sons married Orpah and me, women of Moab. We were happy and I grew to love Naomi, my mother-in-law.

"Then we seemed to be cursed, for both Mahlon and Chilion died. How bitter life was; Naomi had neither husband nor sons.3 She heard that in her land God had visited the people and given them food, so she decided to return there. She felt that it would be better to be in her own country, rather than our land. Naomi, Orpah, and I started toward the land of Judah, but then Naomi said, 'Go back, each of you, to your mother's house!4 May the Lord be kind to you as you were to the departed and to me! May the Lord grant each of you a husband and a home in which you will find rest.'5 She kissed us good-bye and all three of us loudly wept. 'Go back, my daughters! Why should you come with me? Have I other sons in my womb who may become your husbands? Go back.... my lot is too bitter for you, because the Lord has extended his hand against me.' Orpah kissed Naomi and then obeyed her words, but I just couldn't leave even though Naomi scolded me for staying.6 I said, 'Do not ask me to abandon or forsake you! for wherever you go I will go, wherever you lodge I will lodge, your people shall be my people, and your God my God. Wherever you die I will die, and there be buried.'7

"Naomi saw that Orpah needed to make her own choice and I needed to make my own choice. All three of us loved and respected each other, but we each had to choose for ourselves. I was clear and determined, so my mother-in-law stopped trying to change my mind.8 You wonder why I would stay with the elderly rather than go as Orpah. I am not completely sure why I did it. I am not heroic, but I knew I was gaining something in being with someone who had lived so long. Oh, right at that time she was a bitter and cross old woman, but there was much more to the Naomi that I had known over the years. She often had told me of her God, a God of loving kindness, a God who cared for widows and for aliens, a faithful God. In Moab, we had many goddesses and gods, they gave us children and made the land fertile, but Naomi's God seemed more than that." [She gestures as she says the following.] "Her God seemed like one who would hug you and hold you close against her breasts, like one who would shelter you under the shadow of her wings, and care for you when you were old and gray.9 Naomi spoke of Abraham and Sarah who dared go to a strange country,

and I felt their God giving me courage to go to a strange country. Husbands can make love, but they don't always understand how a woman feels, what a woman thinks. I cherish this friendship with a woman, this friendship with an older person. I cherish Naomi, with whom I can talk.

"When we came to Bethlehem there was much interest. Some of the women remembered the Naomi who had left.10 Work, time, and grief had changed her. They asked, 'Can this be Naomi?' Naomi means sweetness." [She sits and sags over like a tired old woman.] "My mother-in-law replied, 'Do not call me Naomi. Call me Mara, bitter, for the Almighty has made it very bitter for me. I went away with an abundance, but Shaddai has brought me back destitute.'"11 [She stands and continues.]

"It happened to be the time of the barley harvest and the laws here say that the poor may follow the reapers and glean and keep whatever little is left.12 I was doing that when I heard the owner of the estate ask one of his overseers, 'Whose girl is this?' Men did not ask who I was; they asked to what man did I belong. As a widow and as one with no relatives here, I knew if the workers or the owner wanted to molest me there was no one to stop them. Even if they don't molest you they often taunt, 'Hey, widow, what did you do that God should punish you with the death of your husband?' Also I did not know that being a foreigner was going to be so hard. In Moab, Naomi never told me that many people of Judah think marrying a woman of another country brings the wrath of God.13 They say, 'Our God is above all other gods,' and often they act like they are above all other peoples.

"But I praise the God who cares for widows, for orphans, and for aliens. The owner of this field did not ask to whom I belonged to see if he could take advantage of me. In fact, he told me to work among his own women servants, and he told the young men not to harm me. He said, 'I have had a complete account of what you have done for your mother-in-law after your husband's death; you have left your father and your mother and the land of your birth, and have come to a people whom you did not know previously. May the Lord reward what you have done! May you receive a full reward from the Lord, the God of Israel, under whose wings you have come for refuge.'14 He not only blessed me, but he shared lunch. Later, I overheard him tell his workers to just let some handfuls of grain fall on the ground so that I could pick them up." [She acts as if she is diligently picking up grain and putting it in a basket.] "When I got home I had plenty of food for Naomi, both leftovers from the lunch and from what I gleaned. I told her about the kind man. She must have been praying for me. When I told her the man's name was Boaz, her eyes brightened." [She sits and speaks like Naomi.] "She said, 'Why he is a relative of ours, one of our next of kin. You keep working in his field, in other places you might be molested or insulted.' I didn't know that we had any relatives.

"Daily, we had enough grain to live, but when it came to the end of the barley and wheat harvests I was afraid again. If I were a man there would have been many ways to survive, to work, to protect this precious one with gray hairs. But what Naomi lacked in strength to support herself, she made up for by her wisdom and her cleverness.[15] Whether or not it is right for things to be this way for women, she knew the only tool available for a woman, she knew how to use the only power, the only means a woman had, and she told me what to do.[16]

"Naomi explained the law of Israel to me, the law that was to protect people like us. The law was a part of God's covenant, a way of manifesting the loving kindness of God. She said, 'If a man dies, his brother is to marry the widow. If there are no brothers, the next of kin are urged to fulfill the duty.' Though Naomi had come back to this place of their family, none of the men had made any effort in either justice or charity to live out the covenant. No man of the town imaged God, the redeemer, and became a redeemer for the house of Elimelech, a redeemer for Naomi and for me.[17] But Naomi, woman of prayer, woman who knew the laws of protection, woman who imaged her God, this Naomi, cared about me. Even if men were not protectors of her, she wanted to be a protector of me. She said, 'I must seek a home for you that will please you. Now, is not Boaz, with whose servants you were, a relative of ours?'

"As I said before, Naomi knew the only power we women had.[18] She continued, 'This evening he will be winnowing barley at the threshing floor. So bathe and anoint yourself; then put on your best attire and go down to the threshing floor. Do not make yourself known to the man before he has finished eating and drinking. But when he lies down, take note of the place where he does so. Then go, uncover the lower part of his body, and lie down. He will tell you what to do.' I said, 'I will do whatever you advise,' and I did." [She stands and gestures initiating the celebration.] "All happened as she said it would—they had a big celebration after the plentiful harvest, Boaz had much to eat and much to drink, and then he went to sleep in a corner behind a big pile of grain. I slipped over and quietly uncovered him and I lay there as she said. I remembered her words, 'He will tell you what to do.'[19] I thought perhaps I should tell him what to do. I

remembered that first day in the field when he had prayed and blessed me, 'May you receive a full reward from the Lord, the God of Israel, under whose wings you have come for refuge.' I thought if one prays that another might be sheltered and find refuge, and the person who prays has the means to shelter the one in need, their prayer is empty if they do not embody what they ask of God. So, as I lay there on the floor beside Boaz, I decided that I should challenge him to fulfill his prayer, and to live up to the laws of the covenant calling for care of a departed one's family.

"In the middle of the night he awoke. He was startled to find me there and himself in this position. He asked, 'Who are you?' I said, 'I am your servant Ruth. Spread the corner of your cloak over me, for you are my next of kin.' He was willing to accept my challenge, and seemed pleased that I would come to him an older relative. He said, 'Be assured, daughter, I will do for you whatever you say; all my townspeople know you for a worthy woman. Now, though indeed I am closely related to you, you have another relative still closer. Stay as you are for tonight, and tomorrow, if he wishes to claim you, good! let him do so. But if he does not wish to claim you, as the Lord lives I will claim you myself. Lie there until morning.'

"We rose before people would be able to see us and Boaz generously filled my cloak with six measures of barley. [She stands with her profile to the people, and holds out her dress as if it is filled with grain, but also hinting at pregnancy. The writer seems to use this gesture of giving her seed as a literary foreshadowing of her pregnancy. The visuals of this can suggest that.] I returned to Naomi, both happy and afraid. I told her that Boaz was willing to wed me, but he said that another relative had first rights. She said just to wait, she was sure he would soon take care of this.

"Boaz went to the city gates where men do business, and he gathered ten elders as one does to witness a legal transaction." [She mimics the men's deep voices.] "He found the relative and he said, 'Naomi, the widow of Elimelech has some land. You as the next of kin have the first right to get it. Do you want to claim the property?' The man said, 'Yes, I want to claim the land.' Then Boaz said, 'And with the land one would need to take the widowed daughter of Mahlon—she's a Moabite woman—and raise up children to carry on the name of Elimelech on his land.'[20] [This should invite humor as the man's true self is revealed.] "The man changed. He wanted land; he did not want a widowed wife, a wife who was a *Moabite, a foreigner*. He did not want to be a redeemer. He did not want the responsibility of children whose credit went to another. The man said, 'No, no, I do not think I want the land. You may claim the property.' [She laughs with delight and changes from the man's brusque voice back to a warm, feminine tone. The next section is also humorous, but in a different way.]

"And so Boaz and I were married."

(She leaves and puts on a full-length apron that has been padded to look like she is pregnant. A lullaby is softly strummed in the background. She walks in slowly and heavily, as if she were in the ninth month, and she has a big smile. She sits down.)

"God has blessed Boaz and me. This is a very special time for me." [She picks up the lemon and the apple and thoughtfully continues.] "As I wait these months, I have a chance to look back over my life, all the times of sweetness and the times of bitterness. God has been with me through it all. Who would ever think that one who chose to stay with an old woman would now...." [She rubs her stomach and smiles.] "God is good."

(She stands walks to the back, turns around, slightly bends forward as if in pain, and converts the apron to a baby cradled in her arms. She turns back around with a big smile.)

"Isn't little Obed precious? He looks a little like his grandmother." [She sits and shows the baby the lemon and the apple and talks to him.] "You also will find that sometimes life is sweet and sometimes life is bitter. Naomi loves to hold Obed and she is his nurse. The women here say to Naomi, 'Blessed is "El Shaddai" who has not failed to provide you today with an heir! May he become famous in Israel! He will be your comfort and the support of your old age, for his mother is the daughter-in-law who loves you. She is worth more to you than seven sons!'[21] The women say that I, a woman, am worth more than seven sons to Naomi. I want to tell you that Naomi is worth more than seven fathers to me—how blessed it is to have the friendship of a woman like this. Naomi has imaged the God of Israel, the God under whose wings I have been given refuge." [The song "El Shaddai" is sung as she sits gently rocking the baby.]

(The ministers and the storyteller bring out plates of little slices of sweet fruit, such as apples or peaches, and bitter fruit, such as lemon or lime. One of each can be put on a toothpick. The three hold them up so that everyone may see them, and then they are placed on the table.)

**First:** Gracious God, El Shaddai, we also have known sweetness and bitterness in our lives, in our world. Bless what is sweet; bless what is bitter. Tasting both brings wisdom. May we not be afraid to taste life to the full, for you shelter us under your wings and you give us companions along the way.

**Second:** Let us take time to taste the sweet and the bitter and to remember our lives, the sweet and the bitter parts.

(The fruit is passed for everyone to take and eat. Napkins may be passed first if people would mind sticky fingers. The song "El Shaddai" is softly sung during this.)

**First:** El Shaddai, we thank you for the companions you give us along the bitter and sweet ways of our lives. Let us say aloud or in the depths of our hearts the older companions, like Naomi, for whom we are grateful. (Pause for people to mention names.) Let us say aloud or in the depths of our hearts the younger companions, like Ruth, for whom we are grateful. (Pause for these names.) We thank you for all these companions, living and dead.

(The service can be ended with a blessing to "El Shaddai," or with a gospel reading and song.)

### First Option: Closing Blessing

**Storyteller:** Ruth and Naomi manifested God's love and blessing for each other. They were like God who shelters us under the shadow of her wings. Let us pray for God's blessings as we close. Watch our gestures, then turn to a partner and do the same. The person on the right will give the blessing first, then as the chorus is repeated, the person on the left will bless. (The chorus of "El Shaddai" and the movements described in the Appendix are used.)

### Second Option: Gospel Reading and Song

**Second:** We have heard a story about two widows who in the bitterness of their lives were needy and almost helpless. So often women's status has depended on being related to a man, a father or a husband. Scripture again and again uses the term "widow" to indicate the most powerless and needy. So often in our world today, we feel powerless in the face of bitterness, suffering, evil, injustice, and violence. Naomi was a very wise widow who figured out a way to improve things. Ruth was a very bold widow who took initiative. Let us listen to the story of another wise and bold widow. (She gestures for people to stand and turns to face the first minister at the altar.)

**First:** (She takes the Bible from on the altar, holds it up, and begins the reading which the storyteller and the second minister dramatize. This is a humorous story and it should be read and dramatized with the exaggeration of a comedy.) A reading from the holy gospel according to Luke. (Pause) Once there was a judge in a certain city who respected neither God nor persons. A widow in that city kept coming to him saying....

**Storyteller:** (She angrily walks over to the second minister and knocks on an imaginary door trying to get attention.) "Give me my rights against my opponent." (She continues to knock, and finally freezes in an angry position.)

**First:** For a time he refused, but finally he thought...

**Second:** (She looks at the audience with frustration.) I care little for God or people, but this widow is wearing me out. I am going to settle in her favor or she will end by doing me violence. (Luke 18:2-15, NAB adapted)

(The storyteller put her hands on her hips and looks up with a big, satisfied smile.)

**First:** This is the good news.

**Storyteller:** "Let us learn from these wise, bold widows, let us learn their dance. We encounter difficulties in our world, let us knock persistently." [She humorously demonstrates the gestures to the song "Judge's Dilemma," by Colleen Fulmer, which may be found in the Appendix.] "Those of you on my side of the room are invited to be the widow and follow me knocking." [She knocks, stamps her feet, shakes her arms.] "Those of you on the judge's side of the room, follow the judge with closed ears, closed door, and hard heart." [The "judge" holds her ears, holds up the door, shakes her head "no."] "These are the things the widow wants, repeat them after me now, and then sing them as you learn them, 'Justice for all people, peace in every land, food to feed her children, freedom just to stand—with no more fear of deadly weapons, corporate, structured plans, *and no more war.*'" [This is sung and danced. It is fun and can be even funnier if the widow gestures for the "widows" to "start moving in on" the "judges" in the second-to-last verse.]

**First:** Go forth, work for justice and peace, (wink at the people) and be wise and bold like these widows.

# For Further Reflection, Journalizing, and/or Discussion

Scriptural Background: The Book of Ruth

## Questions

1. Have you had older friends? What have you learned from them?

2. Sometimes life and pain make us feel bitter and angry with God. How can we deal with these feelings?

3. Ruth came to know the God of Judah and Israel through Naomi and her family, If we lived in a place where people had never heard of the Judeo-Christian God, could these people come to know God through us? What sort of God shines through us?

4. What types of people are the objects of discrimination in our society? What would have happened to Naomi if she would have been prejudiced against living with a foreigner, which Ruth was?

5. So often through the ages, women's physical appeal has been the only power available to them. How can this overemphasis on the physical be bad for both individuals and for society? How can women learn to develop and value not just the physical but also other parts of themselves? How would men feel if they had to spend a great deal of time and money on impractical and uncomfortable clothing, shoes, and makeup? How do you feel about the expectations that women should appear attractive?

6. Boaz prayed that Ruth might be blessed by the God of Israel under whose wing she had come for rest (Ruth 2:12). How have we known a God as a mother bird who shelters and protects us?

7. A mother eagle teaches her young to fly by taking them on her back and then swooping down allowing the young to fly alone. God empowers us that way. Naomi empowered Ruth by setting her free to go home. How can we learn to free and empower others?

8. Having to take full responsibility for decision-making is difficult for many widows. How can we learn to consider different possibilities, seeking counsel when necessary, then make and live with our own decisions?

9. Today, being a widowed or single woman can still be an economic tragedy. How can societies learn to value and justly compensate work done by women?

### Readings

Widows who image God in their generosity and desire for justice:

• The widow who fed and cared for God's prophet (I Kgs. 17:7)

• The widow who gave all she could (Mark 12:41-44)

• The widow who called David to justice (II Sam. 14:4-17)

• The widow who confronted an unjust judge (Luke 18:1-8)

Women whose only power was physical charm:

• Tamar seeks to have a child (Gen. 38)

• Judith overcomes the enemy (Judg. 16:3-9)

• Esther woos the king to save her people (Esther 4)

• An older and a younger woman who help each other (Luke 1:39- 56)

# Reflections on the Development and Use of the Service

The 117-year-old group of sisters to which I belong (an active American congregation coming from a 361-year-old contemplative French group of nuns) has diminished in North America. Our average age is over sixty-five and we have had few younger members. A decision was made to combine our decreasing American provinces. At our last assembly before the merger, there was some grief and anger. I shared a variation of this service. Among our sisters there has been a major concern whether young members will remain in the group to take care of the elderly. Among the young there has been a concern if the elderly will accept younger persons "as they are." Younger persons are like Ruth, "foreigners, aliens," who do not always conform to the customs of the older group. The service closed with all of us, young and old, people of different countries and different ideas, holding each other. Many were in tears after this powerful ritual which named our pain, but also our hope. Scholars are considering which biblical stories are told by women in contrast to stories about women told by men. Can contemporary women's spontaneous identification with a story give us some clues of what stories were more likely women's stories in biblical times? This story of Ruth has more of the straight scriptural text (only put in first-person) than any other story in this collection. The other stories needed much of what Elisabeth Schussler Fiorenza calls "historical imagination" to reconstruct them as women's stories. There may have been male editors of Ruth, particularly in the writing of the male genealogy at the end, but almost all of the story seems to come from women storytellers. The responses I have received from contemporary women who strongly and spontaneously identify with it lead me to believe this.

# Chapter 7
# Susanna, a Voice for the Vulnerable

## Themes

• Recognizing people's plans to exploit

• Recognizing that the story of the weak may not be believed when in conflict with the stories of those who have power or prestige

• Remembering God who calls us to truth

• Remembering strong women of other ages

• Refusing to be exploited, though the consequences may be death

## Possible Uses

• Lent; reconciliation services

• With lectionary reading of the fifth Sunday of Lent, Cycle A; the fifth week of Lent; with *An Inclusive Language Lectionary*, alternative reading for the twelfth Sunday of Pentecost, Cycle B

• For analysis of oppressive structures, legal protection for weaker peoples, rape prevention programs, support of victims of sexual violence

## The Service

(Chairs are arranged in a semicircle with a table and small stool on one side. The table should have a cloth in a color that relates to the storyteller's dress, a vase for the flowers she will bring, a Bible, and candles. Some verses of the round, "Passionate God," by Colleen Fulmer, which can be found in the Appendix are sung. The gestures given there may be used.)

**First Minister:** We do not always hear the stories of the vulnerable, the exploited, and the oppressed. We do not always listen to the cries of the deep, vulnerable, and oppressed parts of ourselves.

(This service can be used to pray with any people who are exploited, or it may have a particular focus. For instance, it has been used on the anniversary [4 December] of the four American women who were killed in El Salvador as a way of praying in solidarity with all who question the exploitation of the poor in Latin America. A slide show of people there and a tape of refugees' voices was used as an introduction to the service. Information on exploitation in South Africa has been used. At a women's conference in which there was a collection for a rape crisis center, information about rape and about the center were shared. The service could begin by hearing stories from people who are sometimes not listened to or believed [refugees, exploited workers], or by reading some facts about them. The litany given in the service on Hagar could be a source for this.)

**Second Minister:** Let us rise and pray. (Pause) God of power, God of gentleness, God of truth, we gather in communion with all the "little ones" whom you love in a special way and in communion with prophets, martyrs, and saints through the ages. As we listen to stories of those have refused to be exploited, open our hearts and give us steadfast faith, undaunted courage, and persevering strong love. This we pray in the name of Jesus Christ, who dared to live and speak the truth. Amen. (She gestures for all to be seated.)

**First Minister:** The biblical tradition of about 2400 years ago tells a story of a person in a position of weakness, who refused to be exploited, to be oppressed, by those who had power. Then, as now, a refusal to accept exploitation may bring death. Let us listen to a contemporary reflection on the story of Susanna from the Book of Daniel.

(The first part of the song "Be Near Me, O God" is softly sung by a soloist, and as it fades the storyteller enters. She carries one or a few lilies and some greenery which she admires then puts in an earthenware vase on the table as she mentions the meaning of her name.)

**Storyteller:** "People call me Susanna, 'beautiful lily.' God has given me beauty.[1] In the land of Babylon, I lived in peace and joy with my husband, Joachim, and our children.[2] God was good to us and I tried to show my gratitude through fidelity to the law which my parents had taught me. Joachim and I were blessed with a fine house and a lovely garden which gave me great pleasure." [She points to the lilies from the garden.] "In the heat of midday I would go to the garden, enjoy its shade and solitude, and bathe in the cool waters of the pond there." [Her tone changes from one of light joy to seriousness.] "Two of the elders, who had been appointed judges to rule our people that year, would come very often to visit my husband.[3] I know I should have been honored that these men, important in the eyes of God and the nation, should come to our home, yet, the way their eyes rested on me, the way they seemed to stare at my body, made me ill at ease.

"One beautiful spring day, I went to the garden at midday as was my custom. It was so hot that I wanted to bathe so I asked my two maidservants to bring me oil and soap."[4] [She sits down as if enjoying the water, then suddenly looks terrified. When she speaks for the men, her voice is deep and cold.] "I was just beginning to enjoy the cool of the water when I could see two figures above me reflected in it. I gasped, my body tensed in fear. I heard a deep voice, 'Look, the garden doors are shut, and no one can see us; give in to our desire, and lie with us. If you refuse, we will testify against you that you dismissed your maids because a young man was here with you.'[5] I turned and looked in terror." [She struggles with fear and confusion as she speaks.] "The voices were the voices of the leaders of our people, of the two judges elected that year to see that God's laws were kept and that justice was done. If these were the outcasts I could have better believed my ears, but these were the upright, these were the men to whom all look for leadership. I was confused. These are leaders who are to guide one in the paths of good. These are men who are strong, and I am a woman who is weak. This is the voice of age, and I have only the inexperience of youth. What did I do wrong that this should befall me?[6] How can this treacherous act seem all right in their eyes? And if I do not submit, there is nothing but stoning for me. Who would ever believe the words of a woman against the evidence of men of importance? Who would ever believe the voice of a lowly one against the voices of those who are the leaders?"

[She stands. She gestures like the girl being stoned trying to protect her face and her body.] "Have I served my God faithfully all my life only to now be abandoned and stoned? for such is the punishment of women who have been caught in adultery.[7] I'd seen it once. She was small and lovely, no more than seventeen, and she stood there screaming, 'But it wasn't my fault.' As the stones began to break her flesh and as blood ran down her face, her voice weakened, but she kept saying, 'But it wasn't my fault.' My heart quaked

at the thought of being stoned, yet, I know that I have not done anything wrong in the eyes of God." [She stands tall and gets stronger and stronger as she remembers other women.] "Where is the God of Sarah, Rachel, and Leah, the God of Deborah, Esther, and Ruth? I remembered Deborah who was a prophetess, a judge and leader of the people, Deborah who stood up against the enemies of God when strong men were afraid to do so. I remembered Esther who spoke up for our people though she knew doing so was risking her own life.[8] Would the God of Deborah and of Esther, the God who had loved me and blessed me, the God of truth, be with me in the face of these evil men?

"I sighed and said, 'I am completely trapped, if I yield, it will be my death; if I refuse, I cannot escape your power. Yet, it is better for me to fall into your power, rather than let you exploit me.'" [She holds up her hand, palm forward and speaks firmly.] "'No, no.' And I screamed as loud as I could. The people from the house rushed to my cry, but before I could speak, the men told them they had caught me in adultery."[9] [She turns, hunches over in sorrow and walks away. As she does this, the first verse of "Be Near Me, O God" is sung. She puts a shawl around her head and shoulders. As the music fades away, she fearfully walks back.]

"The next day, the two elders, those that had gathered to judge me, and all the people came to our house. They called me, and I came veiled and weeping. My husband and children, my parents and all my relations came with me. The two judges had them take off my veil, the wretches wanted to feast their eyes on me."[10] [She lets her shawl fall down to the floor and stands there very vulnerably.] "If they could have, in their vindictiveness they would have totally disrobed my body which they could not have in the garden. My people wept with me, and I turned my heart to God, who hears the pleas of the innocent. But it was only the elders who had a chance to speak. 'As we were walking in the garden alone, this woman entered with two girls and shut the doors of the garden, and dismissed the girls. A young man, who was hidden there, came and lay with her. When we in a corner of the garden saw this crime, we ran toward them. We saw them lying together, but the man we could not hold, because he was stronger than we; he opened the doors and ran off. Then, we seized this one and asked who the young man was, but she refused to tell us. We testify to this.'

"Since they were judges, their words were believed and I was condemned to death. Then I prayed, 'O eternal God, you know what is hidden and are aware of all things before they come to be: you know that they have testified falsely against me. Here I am about to die, though I have done none of the things with which these wicked men have charged me.' I began to wonder if there were a God, and the people began to lead me to the place for stoning." [She starts to walk away, then stops.] "As we started to go my God answered. A young man called Daniel was the voice of my God.

"Daniel came forward and shouted, 'I am innocent of the blood of this woman.' The people turned and asked what he meant. He said, 'Are you such fools, O Israelites! To condemn a woman of Israel without examination and without clear evidence? Return to court, for they have testified falsely against her.' So the people went back." [This should invite humor. She goes to one side, imitates Daniel, and then the lecherous old man.] "Daniel separated the two elders and he said to the first, 'Now, then, if you were a witness, tell me under what tree you saw them together.' The man said, 'Under a mastic tree.' David put the first judge aside and then he called the other one." [She goes to the other side, imitates Daniel, and then a nervous, lecherous old man.] "David asked the other, 'Under what tree did you see them together?' The second man said, 'Under an oak.' Daniel rejoiced and said that their own lies had trapped them and the angel of God was waiting to punish them. All the people shouted, blessing God who saved me. The people turned against the elders. My life was spared. My mother and father, my husband and children and all our relations thanked the God of the weak, the God of the innocent, the God of truth."[11] [She stands tall and relieved, but then hesitates to rejoice as she continues.]

"Yet, I still wonder about the girl whom I saw stoned, the one who was only about seventeen. The people had *heard* that she was committing adultery— the young girl who kept crying, 'But it wasn't my fault, but it wasn't my fault.' No one listened to her story, no one believed her story." [She walks away pondering as the second verse of "Be Near Me, O God" is sung, and there is some time for meditation.]

**Second Minister:** As Susanna was weak, so we are all weak and vulnerable in some ways.[12] As the elders were in positions of power and authority, so we all are powerful in some ways. As the prophet Daniel, we are all called to come between the weak and the powerful and search for truth and justice.

(This can be written in a program, explained now, or both. "Those of us who were born in the first third of the year, January to April, are invited to 'be Susanna,' that is the weak, and pray in their name. Those of us who were born in the second third of the year, May to August, are invited to 'be the elders,' those in power and pray in their name. Those of us who were born in

the last third of the year, September to December, are invited to 'be Daniel,' those who come between the weak and the powerful and to pray in their name." Or, people can be divided by sections of the room or rows.)

**Second Minister:** Let us join in an embodied prayer. Those of you who are weak, like Susanna, are invited to come to the center and kneel, sit, or squat on the floor, and from this low position, this weak position, voice your prayers. (After they have come forward and gotten on the floor, the minister continues.) Let those of us who recall the weak speak our prayers. (Usually people speak up spontaneously, but, if desirable, a few people can be prepared for this with prayers, such as: "For the children of the world"; "For disabled persons"; "For the sexually abused." This should not be rushed, and some silence in these positions of prayer can be meaningful.) Now the second group, the people like the elders, are invited to come and stand tall and powerful in a circle around, looking down on those who are weak. (People may laugh as they do this, but that is all right. Though they may feel strange at first, the movement invites people to really ponder positions of weakness and strength in the world.) Let those of us who recall the powerful speak our prayers. (There are spontaneous prayers, such as: "For all of us in the United States, the most powerful nation in the world"; "For those who teach children and thus shape the future of the world"; "For judges and police"; "For the leaders of our church"; "For those who control nuclear weapons.") Now, the last group of you are invited to stand between the weak and the powerful; you, like Daniel, come between the weak and the powerful. You may have to push your way in between—that happens in the world too! (After they have done this, the prayer continues.) Let those of us who recall those who come between the weak and the powerful, searching for truth and justice, speak our prayers. (There are spontaneous prayers, such as: "For those who try to protect refugees"; "For people who try to reconcile families that are fighting"; "For those who lobby for the needy"; "For those who do community organizing." After spoken prayer and some reflective silence, this continues.)

**First Minister:** In the Susanna story in scripture, she is freed and the elders are killed. Yet, we do not pray that the powerful be killed; in fact we, are aware that we are a part of the most powerful nation. Let us stand not above or below each other, but remember that we are all sinners and that we are all graced. Let us hold hands in a circle together, promising to challenge and to help each other, and to listen to each other's stories. The powerful might help the weak up! (Pause until all are standing in a circle.) Let us listen to a gospel story of another women who sought truth. Our God is like the woman who continues to demand justice. Let us pray that we may not be hard-hearted like the judge.

**Second Minister:** (She takes the Bible from the table, stands in the circle, holds it up, and reads dramatically, bringing out the humor of this determined woman and worn-out judge.) A reading from the holy gospel according to Luke.

"Once there was a judge in a certain city who respected neither God nor people. A widow in that city kept coming to him saying, 'Give me my rights against my opponent.' For a time he refused, but finally he thought, 'I care little for God or man, but this widow is wearing me out. I am going to settle in her favor or she will end by doing me violence.' The Lord said, 'Listen to what the corrupt judge has to say. Will not God then do justice to the chosen who call out day and night? Will God delay long over them, do you suppose? I tell you, God will give them swift justice. But when the Human One comes, will he find any faith on the earth?'"

(Pause) This is the good news (adapted from Luke 18:2-8, NAB).

**Storyteller:** Let us learn to knock persistently. (She humorously demonstrates the gestures to the song "Judge's Dilemma," by Colleen Fulmer, which may be found in the Appendix.) Those of you on my side of the room are invited to be the widow and follow me knocking. (She knocks, stamps her feet, shakes her arms.) Those of you on the other side of the room, follow the judge with closed ears, closed door, and hard heart. (One of the ministers as the "judge" holds her ears, holds up the door, shakes her head "no.") These are the things the widow wants, repeat them after me now, and then sing them as you learn them, 'Justice for all people, peace in every land, food to feed her children, freedom just to stand—with no more fear of deadly weapons, corporate, structured plans, *and no more war*.'" [This is sung and danced. It is fun and can be even funnier if the widow gestures for the "widows" to "start moving in on" the "judges" in the second-to-last verse.]

### First Option for Closing

**First Minister:** Go forth, like this brave woman Susanna, like this bold widow, speak for truth and justice—and remember when God, like the widow, knocks at your hard heart, let her in!

("Choose Life" or "Passionate God" by Colleen Fulmer, found in the Appendix, may be sung with gestures.)

### Second Option for Closing

**First Minister:** God wishes to bring justice. Do we have faith? Will we cooperate with God in bringing justice? Let each of us decide in the depths of our hearts how we might cooperate with God.

(The participants may be invited to do one of the following: [1] to write in their spiritual journals or on a piece of paper their reflections and resolutions; [2] to get in pairs or small groups and discuss their reflections on the stories and prayer; [3] to sign pledges, letters, etc., in support of those who are in weak positions; [4] to make financial contributions to a related cause.)

**Second Minister:** Let us rise and pray. (Pause) God of Susanna, of Deborah, and of Esther, God of the poor and the innocent, God of truth, may the stories we have heard take root in our hearts and begin to grow and bloom like lilies. May those we have remembered today strengthen us to work for justice and peace. This we ask in the name of Jesus, who lives and reigns forever and ever. Amen.

("Choose Life" or "Passionate God," by Colleen Fulmer, found in the Appendix, may be sung with gestures.)

## For Further Reflection, Journalizing, and/of Discussion

Scriptural Background: Dan. 13

### Questions

1. Many of us have experiences of a system of power or a person in power trying to take advantage of us in some way. We may wish to protect their reputations, but when is it better to reveal an unjust situation?

2. Why is it important to hear stories from different perspectives?

3. How can people begin to refuse to be economically raped as Susanna refused to be physically raped? How can exploited workers of different countries begin to unite in resistance to economic exploitation?

4. More and more studies indicate that rape is not motivated by sex drives which cannot be controlled; rape is motivated by a desire to display one's power when one is insecure. How can we begin to learn to share power and to embrace nonviolence?

5. Victims of rape and other crimes are often blamed for what has happened to them. How can we learn to place responsibility in the right places?

6. What assistance can your church or community offer to persons who have suffered from rape, incest, marital rape, or other sexual harassment?

7. Today, gigantic systems (e.g., sexism, militarism, colonialism, racism, heterosexism, ageism) loom as large as the two elders over the vulnerable Susanna. What other stories do we know of people who are like Susanna in refusing to be exploited?

8. Daniel said, "I am innocent of the blood of this woman," as Pontius Pilate said of Christ. When the innocent suffer, do we as Pilate wash our hands and ignore it, or do we as Daniel step forward and try to right the injustice? In what ways is Susanna like Christ?

9. How can scriptural stories of rape and the abuse of women help us confront rape, marital rape and the sexual abuse of women and children today? Do we hear as much preaching and teaching against sexual harassment of women and a lack of male responsibility for the results of sexual activity as we hear against abortion? How do both of these deal with respect for life and quality of life?

### Readings

Sexual abuse of women:

• Raping Dinah offends the men who possess her (Gen. 34:1-31)

• David takes another's wife (II Sam. 11)

• David's son rapes his sister and David seems to sympathize with the son (II Sam. 13:1-2)

• Absalom rapes his father's concubines to insult his father (II Sam. 16:15-22)

• Lot is willing to let his daughters be raped to save his guests (Gen. 19:8)

• A Levite throws out his concubine to be raped to save himself (Judg. 19:1-30)

• Men of Israel rape six hundred women to avenge the rape of the concubine (Judg. 21:12-24)

## Reflections on the Development and Use of the Service

This is an emotionally charged story and one that can easily anger or polarize people. While I have used other stories alone or in variety of prayer experiences, I have always used the "three-level prayer," identifying with the victim, the oppressor, and those in between, with this story. This prayer changes the focus from polarizing, from anger toward the oppressor, to an invitation for all of us to conversion, for we are all oppressor, as well as victim. The initial development of the Susanna story was prompted by a priest's attempt to sexually exploit me and by the systematic exploitation of women in society and religions.

I shared the story in a service remembering the four American women killed in El Salvador and others who have suffered in Latin America. Susanna was a metaphor for all those in weak positions who dare to refuse exploitation of themselves or others, even if it will mean death. Over a year after the service, I received a letter from a seminarian who had attended. He wrote the story still haunted him, especially the ending where Susanna asks, "What about the girl who was stoned? She kept saying, 'But it wasn't my fault.' No one listened to her story." His ability to deeply enter into the story reinforces the idea that women's stories need to be heard and that both men and women in the world may find healing in them.

# Chapter 8
# Daughter, Your Faith Has Saved You

## Themes

• Believing that one is unclean or unworthy in some way

• Losing strength in fear or worry

• Feeling the pain of the others' suffering

• Desire to be healed

• Believing in God's power

## Possible Uses

• Lent; healing and anointing services; reconciliation services

• With lectionary readings for the thirteenth Sunday of Ordinary Time, Cycle B; the fourth week of Ordinary Time

• For women's programs; programs on those discriminated against, such as the disabled, homosexuals, the elderly

## The Service

(Participants are seated in a semicircle. The room has low lighting and a cluster of candles on a table near the front. By the candles is an open Bible and one or more containers of oil. When the service has been done with groups of all women who were interested in the relationships between women and ritual [see the fourth chapter for a discussion of this], the women have been invited before the service to write in their spiritual journals or on paper their feelings about their monthly menses. This is not to be shown to anyone, but it helps focus ideas and prayers. The song "A Voice Is Heard in Ramah," by Colleen Fulmer, which may be found in the Appendix, is sung and the presider and readers may lead the people in the movement. The presider gestures for all to be seated and the song is played softly as the first reader speaks.)

**First Reader:** The prophet's grief over the people's suffering

(Jer. 8:18-19a and 20-23 is read.)

**Presider:** We gather in God's presence. We reflect on the wounds of the world, violence among nations, divisions among races, classes, sexes. We reflect on the wounds in our own lives, how our hearts bleed. We reflect on the symbol of blood, a sign of death, a sign of life. We reflect not only on blood, but on women's blood. In primitive cultures, people saw that blood and new life emerged from women's bodies. Primitive people also saw women shed blood through their menses at times when they were not pregnant and giving birth. Blood was associated with life and was considered very precious, sacred. Yet, what was sacred was also considered fearful and frightening. So, women manifested something wonderful yet fearful. The Judeo-Christian tradition revealed this ambivalent attitude toward women's blood and women. Let us listen to words of scripture.

(The mime or storyteller stands in front with her back turned. During the first reading, she stands straight, but during the following ones she begins to get tense, and begins to subtly reveal embarrassment by crouching over.)

**Second Reader:** Readings from the Book of Leviticus.

"Since the life of a living body is in its blood, I have made you put it on the altar, so that atonement may thereby be made for your own lives, because it is the blood, as the seat of life, that makes atonement" (Lev. 17:11, NAB).

**First:** "When a woman has her menstrual flow, she shall be in a state of impurity for seven days. Anyone who touches her shall be unclean until evening. Anything on which she lies or sits during her impurity shall be unclean. Anyone who touches her bed shall wash his garments, bathe in water, and be unclean until evening" (Lev. 15:19-21, NAB).

**Second:** "When a woman is afflicted with a flow of blood for several days outside her menstrual period, or when her flow continues beyond the ordinary period, as long as she suffers this unclean flow she shall be unclean, just as during her menstrual period" (Lev. 15:25, NAB).

**First:** "Tell the Israelites: When a woman has conceived and gives birth to a boy, she shall be unclean for seven days, with the same uncleanness as at her menstrual period. On the eighth day, the flesh of the boy's foreskin shall be circumcised, and then she shall spend thirty-three days more in becoming purified of her blood; she shall not touch anything sacred nor enter the sanctuary till the days of her purification are fulfilled. If she give birth to a girl, for fourteen days she shall be as unclean as at her menstruation, after which she shall spend sixty-six days in becoming purified of her blood" (Lev. 12:2-5, NAB).

(Silent pause. The mime or storyteller moves away.)

**Presider:** What was it like to be considered ritually unclean in Jewish culture? Would an unclean person never be touched, hugged, caressed, or helped? Since the furniture and bed she touched were considered unclean, did people refrain from visiting her house? We know that anyone who touched her would be considered unclean, so laws said that she should not go to public places because there would be a danger of others being contaminated by her. Who are the persons today who are considered unclean? Those with whom we do not wish to associate? Those whose race, or class or sex or sexual preference we do not wish to be near? The ugly, the elderly, the disabled, the mentally handicapped? And when do we know ourselves as one who is unclean? One who is not liked by others or respected by others? When do we imagine that we could not be loved? How have people, how have institutions made us feel unclean, as if we lacked dignity or worth? (Pause)

**Second:** A story from the gospel of Mark.

(The first option, the second option, or the third option may be used alone. Frequently either the first or the second has been used as the gospel proclamation, then the story has followed as the homily.)

### First Option: Mime/Dance for One Woman

(The mime with her back turned stands at the front. Mark 5:21-43 is proclaimed in a combination of speaking, singing and music which elaborate the emotions of the text. When the text says, "There was a woman in the area who had been afflicted....," the mime turns and begins a dance-like mime as the suffering woman.

After Jesus says to her, "Go in peace and be free of this illness," she dances with delight, and finally turns her back as the story continues. When she turns around again she is Jesus, the teacher, listening to the people. She does a dance-like mime as Jesus, and after the daughter of Jarius has been raised to life, there is joyful music as she dances with joy and "Alleluias" begin to be sung. She dances gestures of praise raising her arms. As the music builds, she says, "All of us are the family of the daughters that Jesus raises to life, all of us witness the healings, the resurrections, the transformations. Let us celebrate that life, let us all stand, sing, dance with joy." She leads the participants in simple, repeated gestures raising their arms. As the music fades, she gestures for them to be seated. She may then do all or a shortened version of the story, or the service may continue with the prayers at the end of the story.)

### Second Option: Mime for a Woman and a Man

(This mime focuses on the power of touch, on people who touch us, and on reaching out for touch when we need it. In the first half of the story the woman is the Jesus figure, and in the second half the man is. Sometimes we are "Jesus" for others, and sometimes they are "Jesus" for us. Ministry is not just serving and touching, but a dynamic of letting ourselves be touched, touching, and letting ourselves be touched.... The mimes basically enact the story, but they do it in a simplified, stylized way. The attempt is not to portray detail, but to indicate the relationships and emotions. The mimes stand in front with their backs turned to the congregation.)

**Second:** Now when Jesus had crossed back to the other side again in the boat, a large crowd gathered around him and he stayed close to the lake. (The woman mime as Jesus turns around, steps forward and opens her hands as if preaching.) One of the officials of the synagogue, a man named Jarius, came near. Seeing Jesus, he fell at his feet and made this earnest appeal: (The woman leans forward, listening.) "My little daughter is critically ill. Please come and lay your hands on her so that she may get well and live." The two went off together and a large crowd followed, pushing against Jesus. (The woman takes a few steps and shows difficulty pushing against the crowd. She walks, faces the back, and stands still.)

There was a woman in the area who had been afflicted with a hemorrhage for a dozen years. She had received treatment at the hands of doctors of every sort and exhausted her savings in the process, yet she got no relief; on the contrary, she only grew worse. She had heard about Jesus and came up behind him in the crowd and put her hand to his cloak. (The man mimes as the hemorrhaging woman turns around. He tries to move toward Jesus, but has to strain to do so. He finally kneels behind Jesus and reaches out to touch.) "If I just touch his clothing," she thought, "I shall get well." Immediately, her flow of blood dried up, and the feeling that she was cured of her affliction ran through her whole body. (The man who had been bent over and tense, straightens up and stands tall and free. He takes a few steps away from the woman and stands firmly.) Jesus was conscious at once that healing power had gone out from him. Wheeling about in the crowd, he began to ask, "Who touched my clothing?" (The woman as Jesus turns and looks all around.) His disciples said to him, "You can see how this crowd hems you in, yet you ask, 'Who touched me'? (The man tries to back away, to hunch over and hide.) Despite this, he kept looking around to see the woman who had done it. Fearful and beginning to tremble now as she realized what had happened, the woman came and fell in front of him and told him the whole truth. (The man hesitantly goes to the woman, kneels down, and reaches up in an imploring gesture.) He said to her, "Daughter, it is your faith that has cured you. Go in peace and be free of this illness."

(Slowly, the woman leans over, embraces the man, and raises him up. Then, they stand there for a moment clasping each other's hands and looking at each other. Then, both go to their starting positions with their backs turned. There is a long silent pause. The woman who played Jesus will now play the little girl. The man will play Jesus. The woman goes and inconspicuously lies down on a "bed" of a few chairs placed side by side.)

He had not finished speaking when people from the official's house arrived saying, "Your daughter is dead. Why bother the teacher further?" (The man turns around and listens quietly.) Jesus disregarded the report that had been brought and said to the official: "Fear is useless. What is needed is trust." (The man shakes his head then reaches out to invite trust.) He would not permit anyone to follow him except Peter, James, and James' brother John. As they approached the house of the synagogue leader, Jesus was struck by the noise of people wailing and crying loudly on all sides. He entered and said to them: (The man walks over to near where the woman is lying.) "Why do you make all this din with your wailing? The child is not dead. She is asleep." At this, they began to ridicule him. Then he put them all out. (The man raises his hand and gently but firmly gestures for them to leave. Then, he looks fondly at the family.)

Jesus took the child's father and mother and his own companions and entered the room where the child lay. Taking her hand, he said to her, "*Talitha, koum*," which means, "Little girl, get up." (The man takes the hand of the woman and begins to massage it, then he massages her arm.) The girl, a child of twelve, stood up immediately and began to walk around. (The woman slowly arises, looking at first surprised and then happy.) At this, the family's astonishment knew no bounds. He enjoined them strictly not to let anyone know about it, and told them to give her something to eat. (The woman and man clasp hands and look at each other. They freeze in this position.)

This is the good news (Mark 5:21-43, NAB). (After this, the storyteller may do all or a shortened version of the story, or the service may continue with the prayers at the end of the story.)

### Third Option: Storytelling

(The storyteller walks slowly, sadly up to the front. She might cross her arms over her stomach when she speaks of bleeding.)

**Storyteller:** "I had bled for twelve years. Twelve years of never being touched, for a bleeding woman is unclean, defiled.[1] I had been left out for twelve years. As Leviticus says, the bed a bleeding woman sleeps on is unclean, the furniture she touches is unclean, and a man who touches anything she has touched is unclean.[2] One cannot go where she wants because her very touch would defile another. The people of the town did not like me going out or going to the market because they were afraid of touching me and thus becoming defiled.[3] As much as I needed God's help, I could not go and pray with the assembly in the synagogue; I was unclean. This is the law made by the priests, but how can a human being possibly keep some of their laws?

"I bleed. Was it my body or my heart that was bleeding all those years? We live in a world where there were wars and rumors of wars. The rulers say they wish God's reign of peace and justice. Yet, they seek power at all costs and they use violence. My heart bleeds. We live in constant fear of death. No wonder my woman's heart bleeds. Our blood is to carry on life,[4] not again and again to be poured out in conflicts, not again and again to cover battlefields.

"When I was a child we lived near Bethlehem. The ruler Herod wanted to have all the male babies slain." [She acts as if she were cradling a baby, then her arms are torn open.] "I remember my mother's screams the day the soldiers came and grabbed the baby from her breasts and killed him before her eyes. My heart bleeds. It was not the first time a mother had cried. I had heard of when Babylonians sacked Jerusalem. So many of the children were killed, and the people who were left were taken away. Some were in a refugee camp in Ramah—yes, 'A cry was heard at Ramah, sobbing and loud lamentation! Rachel bewailing her children; no comfort for her, since they are no more.'[5]

"My heart bleeds as I think of the daughters of Israel. We can share in the work of caring for our nation, yet rarely are we noticed as our brothers.[6] Their names are remembered, usually ours are forgotten. Our children bear their names, usually our names are forgotten. And for all our labors, we cannot enter the sanctuary of our God.[7] They call us unclean.

"My heart bleeds." [She gestures as if begging.] "I went to a doctor for help. He tried one thing and then another. I went to another doctor and another. They did not hesitate to take my money, but none could ease my difficulty. I had money at first, but money does not last long with doctors. My heart bleeds, not just for myself—as I waited to see the doctors I looked at those around me. There were lines and lines of them, with diseases of all kinds, the little ones and the old. Most with hardly any money. I wondered about our people, we call ourselves God's people. Can we call ourselves God's people if we do not care for all those who are sick?

"My wound is uncurable—my heart bleeds.[8] I had been hearing of a rabbi named Jesus who healed. Oh, there have been rabbis with miraculous healing powers, but we never heard of any who cured women.[9] We women did not even have courage to ask, for we had no idea that anyone would ever want to cure women. But the women of our village were talking. They said that this man cured the mother-in-law of one of his followers, the man named Simon.[10] I heard that this Jesus had pity, and stretched out his hand and touched a leper. He touched an untouchable one and cured him. I, too, am untouchable."[11] [She uses large gestures of breaking out of bondage and recovering sight.] "This man is proclaiming liberty to captives, recovery of sight to the blind and release to prisoners.[12] I will not be imprisoned in this uncleanness any more. I will not let all my strength leave me. I will not be captive to the opinions of a people who look down on me. I have done nothing wrong. Why should I believe that this affliction is my sin? I will not let others treat me as one unclean, one unworthy, one without dignity.[13]

"But, I did not know how to ask this man. I dared not speak to a man in public. Men feel it is demeaning to speak to women. I did not know words to say. But if he has the power they say, words are not necessary. What is really important is beyond words. I thought, 'If I just touch his clothing, I shall get well.' He was teaching on the outskirts of our town and hundreds struggled to get near to hear his words." [She moves forward and finally kneels down on one knee and reaches out as if she were right behind him.] "There were fewer behind him so I began slipping toward him. Some were people who knew me, and they moved out of my way—they did not want to be near someone unclean. I used all my strength to get near him. When I was finally right behind him, I reached out my hand and it trembled—not a fear of nothing happening, for right before he came here in the Decapolis, he cast out a legion of demons.[14] I trembled, wondering if I really wanted to be cured. My life would no longer be the same. Little is expected of a sick woman, but if one is well....Just then, an important man, the ruler of the synagogue, came and asked Jesus to go cure his daughter. Jesus started to follow him and I knew I could not wait. If I wanted healing, it had to be now.

"I went on. I touched the tassel of his cloak.[15] Immediately, I felt the flow of blood dry up. The feeling that I was cured of my affliction ran through my whole body." [She slowly rises and her whole body is stronger and taller than it has been.] "I stood up feeling strong, stronger than I had ever felt. He wheeled about in the crowd asking, 'Who touched my clothing?'[16] His close friends said, 'You can see how this crowd hems you in, yet you ask, "Who touched me?"' "Despite this, he kept looking around to see who had done it. Fearful and beginning to tremble all over as I realized what had happened, I tried to slip away. I did not want people to stare at me. For twelve years, people had known of my illness, of my defilement. Did I again have to be focus of people's disapproval?" [She hides her face.] "Did I have to be stared out and questioned more?

"Again he said, 'Who touched me?' This prophet will know who I am, I cannot hide. Trembling, I came and fell in front of him and told him the whole truth. At first, I felt terrible when he made me say aloud what had happened, but I tell you now because my healing gets stronger and stronger as I speak of the healer. My faith gets stronger and stronger as I speak of that day when I only had a tiny mustard seed of faith, but enough to push through the crowd and touch him.

"He called not to embarrass me because of my illness; he called to proclaim to the whole world that I was not unclean. He was not ashamed to have been touched by me. He was not ashamed for a *woman* to touch his body.[17] He did not say I was unclean. He said I was filled with faith. 'Daughter, it is your faith that has cured you. Go in peace and be free of this illness.'[18] 'Daughter,' he said. Yes, I am a daughter of faith, like Sarah, Leah, Rachel, and Rebecca, a strong daughter like Judith, Ruth, Deborah, and Esther.

"Before Jesus even finished speaking, people from the official's house came and said that his daughter was dead and that there was no need to bother the teacher further. Jesus did not pay attention to them and he said, 'Fear is useless. What is needed is trust.'

"All my years of fear—the twelve years I had bled, the twelve years my heart had bled....I had finally come to trust, to believe. Over the years I've heard stories of another woman who trusted, who believed. Martha's brother Lazarus had died.[19] Jesus asked her if she believed. Yes, she believed that he was the resurrection and the life. She said, 'You are the Messiah, the son of God: he who is to come into the world.'[20]

"Jesus went on to the man's house, and I have heard the story of how he raised the man's daughter, a twelve-year-old.[21] She was twelve, just old enough to have children, to share life, and her life was taken away. Jesus raised me to life on that day, after my twelve years of death—it is death and not life when one's heart is bleeding with fear, with doubt. Jesus is a God of life, a God who pours out his blood to reassure all of us who have bled that such bleeding need not be the end. He was a beginning, a beginning of a new covenant, a covenant marked by his blood." [If there is an altar, she might gesture toward that.] "And those of us who have bled can know the power of his blood." [She walks among the people looking at them and asking them.] "Do you want to touch him? Do you believe? Does your daughter need life? Do you want healing in a war-torn world? Does your heart bleed? Do you know fear is useless, what is needed is trust? Do you dare come near enough to touch this Jesus? Do you really want to be healed?" [After she leaves or is seated, there is a silent pause.)

**Presider:** Oil has been frequently used for healing. Jeremiah seeks a balm in Gilead to heal the daughter of God's people. The Good Samaritan used oil and wine to sooth the wounded person. We have heard stories of a daughter of Israel whose faith in Jesus healed her of her bleeding. We have heard a story of a daughter who was raised to life. We are those healed and resurrected. We are those called to bring to others the healing and life-giving touch of the Christ. Let us stretch our hands over this oil and together bless it. (The presider and/or the readers hold up the oil and all pray silently.) Let us take some of this oil and carefully, gently, and lovingly anoint and massage the hands of another person. Let us pray that we may have faith to touch the Christ and know healing and wholeness. Let us pray that we may touch and bring healing and wholeness to others.

(The presiders and readers begin the anointing and gesture for the others to join. As this is happening, instrumental music, "We Are the Body of Christ," or "Martha's Profession of Faith," by Colleen Fulmer and Rufino Zaragoza, O.F.M. Conv., found in the Appendix, may be used.)

**Presider:** Let us rise and pray that we may embody the words of Isaiah. (Pause)

**First:** Is. 61:1-3a and 6 is read.

**Presider:** May we fulfill that for which we have been healed and given life. May we fulfill the priestly ministry for which we have been called. We pray in the name of Jesus Christ whose touch transforms, and who lives and reigns with the Creator and the Holy Spirit, forever and ever. Amen.

("We Are the Body of Christ" or "Passionate God," by Colleen Fulmer, which may be found in the Appendix, may be sung and danced.)

### A Version of the Service Done with Differently-Abled Persons

(A service based on Mark 5 has been done with differently-abled people designing and doing two dances. An outline of that follows. When people entered, they were told to sit all over the chapel away from and out of touch with others. Instrumental music that was somewhat dissonant and "distant" was used. The programs read:)

### Call to Worship—"Out of Touch," a dance

(A woman in an electric wheelchair had said how often people passed her, and kept their eyes at eye-level not looking down to the level of her wheelchair. It was as if she did not exist; they were "out of touch." She designed her "dance" of moving back and forth across the front of the chapel. Other dancers would walk singly or in small groups toward and by her. Though she would look up with an expectant smile, they would never look down into her eyes. This was done a number of times and the only "music" in the silent chapel was the hum of the electric wheelchair. At the end, the whole congregation read the prayer printed in the program:

Loving God, how often we are far from ourselves, from others, from you.

We pass but do not see each other,
We speak but do not hear each other.
You touch us but we do not feel.
Recreate us with your touch.

Confession and Assurance: "wherewhenwhy?"
a dance about relationships

(Two proficient modern dancers did a dance about relationships in which they yelled each other's names, then even each other's numbers—phone, social-security, zip, street, etc.—trying to find each other. They danced around each other, through each other's legs, on each other's backs, physically touching, yet not "touching," continuing to miss each other's presence.)

**Minister:** You who are far off, come close to our God, for God is full of gentleness and compassion. You who are lonely and out of touch, come near, and be assured you are not alone. (She gestures for all to come sit close to each other and in the front. We had everyone sitting on the floor as a crowd might have sat on a hillside around Jesus. The program then stated, Gen. 2:7, a Creative Touch.)

**Minister:** A reading from the book of Genesis.

"God formed a person out of the dust of the ground and blew into the nostrils the breath of life, and so the person became a living being" (Gen. 2:7,).

(A dance/mime was done by a blind woman crippled with arthritis, and a man. She was on a stool. The man was sort of a formless blob doubled over in front of her. She began to shape him as a lump of clay. He softly groaned as she did this. This was humorous as she felt her own ears to figure out how to shape his. She moved her arms and legs to get an get an idea of how to do his. She counted how many fingers she had to be sure what he needed. She felt the shape of her nose and eyes, then molded his. Finally she breathed over this lump giving him life. He stretched and yawned. She reached for his hands and began to show him how to dance. They danced together in joy. She left having touched and created. There was some music. Then, the story of Mark 5 was done in the second version described above for a woman and a man. The mime was done among the people sitting on the floor as Jesus might have moved and pushed against them. After that there was an opportunity for spontaneous reflections and prayers. All held hands touching each other and sang a chant. Then a joyful circle dance was done. This service could not be re-created, but differently-abled persons can be invited to develop their unique drama and dance for worship. They can proclaim the gospel in powerful ways.)

# For Further Reflection, Journalizing, and/or Discussion

Scriptural Background: Mark 5:21-43

## Questions

1. Who is considered "unclean" or "untouchable" today?

2. Have you ever felt "unclean" or "untouchable?" How can we realize that God wishes to touch us even then?

3. The woman wondered if she really wanted to be healed. Why might people choose to stay ill or to be victims?

4. What situations and problems cause our "hearts to bleed?"

5. "Fear is useless, what is needed is trust." How can we learn to trust ourselves, to trust others, and to trust God?

6. What parts of ourselves need to be healed? What parts of ourselves need to be raised to life?

7. When we are healed by Jesus, how do we carry on his healing mission?

## Readings

Women who are recipients of miracles:

• Widow of Zarephath whose son is restored by Elijah (II Kgs. 17-24)

• Shunammite woman whose son is restored by Elisha (II Kgs. 4:18-37)

• Peter's mother-in-law is cured (Mark 1:29-31)

• Syro-Phoenician woman whose daughter is cured (Mark 7:24-31)

• Widow of Naim whose son is restored by Jesus (Luke 7:11-17)

• Mary of Magdala who is freed of seven demons (Luke 8:2- 3)

• Bent-over woman who is cured (Luke 13:10-17)

• Martha and Mary whose brother is restored (John 11:1- 43)

• A possessed slave girl who is freed (Acts 16:16)

# Reflections on the Development and Use of the Service

In this story, the woman broke a law because she determinedly sought healing. My preaching this story after the gospel in Sunday Eucharist in a Catholic Cathedral was "breaking the law." Canon law states that only the ordained can preach in such circumstances. (One could stretch interpretation and say that telling the story was not "preaching" but drama which does not fit in any category.) This seems to have been the first time a Catholic woman preached there. One of the main ways for the church to find healing and wholeness is for people to continue to "break the laws" which divide the community in the liturgical assembly. Such "breaking of laws" will continue to produce as much scandal and controversy as was produced when the hemorrhaging women and Jesus violated laws that were not life-giving.

Sensitivity to differently-abled persons and to the congregation is needed in incorporating liturgical dance and drama done by the differently-abled for others to watch. Yet, this proved to be extremely moving and effective in this situation. Robert MacAfee Brown, who had a class after this service, began by saying, "How can one have words after an experience like that?" I had invited two differently-abled women to choreograph if they wanted to and whatever they wanted. The two women, one blind and crippled by arthritis and the other confined to a wheelchair, in their determination to get graduate degrees, to be ordained ministers, and to do ministry, personified the woman of the gospel reaching beyond her limitations. The mime with a woman and a man was used, and it makes clear the woman's will to be healed. Yet, the mime presents some deliberate ambiguity in the change of characters. Who brings about the healing? In what way does the healed become the healer? Can women image Jesus? In this situation, how were the differently-abled imaging God and imaging Jesus?

In regard to all of the services in this collection, differently-abled people have been invited to participate and this has been a good learning experience for many of us who are getting sensitive to including women, but still have not overcome exclusive attitudes toward other marginal groups. While some differently-abled have not been able to dance in a circle, they have done gestures. Sometimes groups have gone to hold hands with them and/or to circle them. Physical limitations do not seem to be a problem, but the acknowledgment of them and attitude toward them by leaders and groups have been what matters.

# Chapter 9

# Mary of Magdala, Apostle to the Apostles

## Themes

• Having one's demons of self-doubt dispelled by Jesus' affirmation

• Staying with others through suffering because one has known suffering

• Experiencing the jealousy of others

• Being sent as an apostle though one does not have believable credentials

## Possible Uses

• Easter season, Feast of St. Mary Magdalene (July 22); other holy women's feasts

• Ordination, commissioning for ministry, healing services

## The Service

(The atmosphere of the room should be festive, perhaps with streamers, balloons, flowers, and bright clothes. There is a table covered with a colorful cloth with candles and a Bible. Makeup for the storyteller could be in a basket on the table, but it should be taken off after she has used it. Also pieces of "clown clothes" that could be put over her clothes may be there. The service speaks of two "clown ministers" as well as the storyteller, but four or five clowns can make it even more fun and the parts may be divided among them. Chairs are in a semicircle. People could be given programs similar to the included one which further develops the humor of the service. The story has been done without clown face, but the whole atmosphere of clowning can give insight into resurrection. The storyteller comes out informally in ordinary clothes if possible and speaks.)

**Storyteller:** "You are invited to take a few moments of remembering an experience of death in your life, maybe a physical death, maybe another kind of death."

[Pause] "Now turn to a partner and for a few moments you are invited to share about these experiences." [Pause for the sharing.] "I want to tell you a little about death." [She puts on clown clothes such as a collar, hat, or shirt now or at the end of putting on the makeup. She begins putting on clown whiteface. She needs to practice until she can put on makeup fairly quickly.] "White is the color of death. Corpses turn white. There is a season of the year when we remember those who have died in faith. We often dress up then. Do you know when we remember the dead?" [People will usually say, "Halloween, All Saints Day, All Souls Day." If they do not, the storyteller can tell them.] "And we too must die— but we have already. St. Paul wrote, 'We who are baptized are baptized into his death.' We have died with him." [By now she should have on whiteface and be putting makeup around her eyes.]

"Prophets were people who had big eyes. They could see how very, very much God loved people and they could see people's unfaithfulness. Prophets, like clowns, acted things out. Jeremiah acted out smashing a pot and said that the nation would be smashed like that. Ezekiel laid out on the ground acting out the siege of Jerusalem. People thought he was crazy! Jesus was a prophet who acted things out. What act did he do at his last supper?" [She pauses for an answer.] "Yes, he acted out washing the feet of his disciples. Some people didn't know what to do with that act!" [She draws tear lines on her face.] "Jesus was a prophet who could see how much God loved us and he wept. He wept over Jerusalem. He said, 'As a mother hen longs to gather her chicks under her wings, so I long to gather you.' He wept over his friend Lazarus who died." [She points to her eyes.] "He had big eyes, eyes that could see, eyes that could cry—and those who would follow him need eyes that can see and eyes that can cry...." [She makes up her lips.] "Do you know what this is for?" [She puckers and gives a few kisses.] "'Kiss of Peace' and all that stuff. His followers really get into that 'Kiss of Peace!'" [She touches her face

# "TELL ME WHERE YOU PUT HIM"

### COMEDY
## A ~~TRAGEDY~~ ABOUT
## MAGDALENE
### APOSTLE
## THE ~~PROSTITUTE~~

Illustration 12: Sample progam cover for the service

and thoughtfully remembers the transition from death and sorrow to the joy of clowning.] "White is the color of death...." [She smiles.] "Death, where is your victory? Where is your sting?" [This should go into slapstick humor.]

**First Clown:** [She jumps up, interrupting and questioning the storyteller.] "You can say, 'Where is your sting?' But we have lots of stings, lots of problems, lots of worries, lots of burdens here and now. I've got these great big sins...." [She starts miming as if she were carrying a huge sack. The second clown jumps up interrupting.]

**Second Clown:** "I'll bet I've got more burdens than you." [She mimes even more.] "There's so much junk around."

**Storyteller:** "Okay, everybody I want you to remember those sins, remember those burdens. Let's feel them."

(All three start groaning and miming as if carrying heavy loads. Then they grab huge plastic garbage bags that are hidden under the altar and start throwing in all these burdens. With a little practice, one can get the bag to fill with air. They start to move among the people like garbage collectors. All three of them talk at once.)

**Storyteller:** "Put your burdens right here. Throw in those fears. Stop holding on to your doubts. Give me those sins. Come on. Get rid of all that junk. Sins, sins —any more sins? Hey, I can see you're hiding some of those little anxieties in your back pockets. Throw them away."

(By now the bags are very "heavy." The three of them carry the bags over to one side and throw them out. They wearily come to the center.)

**Storyteller:** "Nothing can separate us from the love of Christ." [Pause.] "Let us open our hearts to hear the good news." [The first clown takes the Bible off the table, holds it up, and then begins to read in a very solemn tone.]

**First Clown:** "A reading from the Holy Gospel according to St. Luke. There was a certain Pharisee who invited Jesus to dine with him. Jesus went to the Pharisee's home and reclined to eat."

**Storyteller:** [She tiptoes over and speaks to the first clown in a very loud whisper.] "That's not the right gospel."

**First Clown:** [She ignores the storyteller and continues.] "A woman known in the town to be a sinner learned that he was dining in the Pharisee's home. She

Illustration 13: Where did you get this stuff of calling the "apostle to the apostles" a loose woman?

brought in a vase of perfumed oil and stood behind him at his feet, weeping so that her tears fell upon his feet. Then...." [Luke 7:36-38, NAB].

**Storyteller:** [She angrily leans over and speaks loudly.] "Stop, that's not the right gospel. That's not the one about Mary Magdalene. I have to preach on it and you aren't even reading the right gospel. You clown, I can't trust you to do anything."

**First Clown:** "Sure it's Mary Magdalene. It says right here 'a woman known to be a sinner,' you know, a loose woman...."

**Storyteller:** "Where did you get this stuff of calling the 'apostle to the apostles' a loose woman?"[1] [She goes over and finds the right text in the scripture and points to it.] "Here, this is the one about Mary Magdalene."

**First Clown:** [She is unhappy.] "Well, before it said seven demons were driven out of Mary Magdalene. What were they if they weren't sexy ones?"

**Storyteller:** "Sex, sex, sex—can't you allow women any other demons? Men can keep their demons and let women name their own demons!"[2]

**First Clown:** Well, okay, but loose women make more sensational art. You know all those paintings and sculptures of Mary Magdalene where she's sort of.... [She mimes a low-cut dress.] "Loose women make more sensational drama and these people like a little drama, don't you?" [She looks to the audience to get response. The storyteller is glaring at her. As the clown starts to read the right gospel, the storyteller quietly moves away and turn her back.] "Well, I'll read the one you said, 'Early in the morning on the first day of the week, while it was still dark, Mary Magdalene came to the tomb. She saw that the stone had been moved away....Mary stood weeping beside the tomb. Even as she wept, she stooped to peer inside, and there she saw two angels in dazzling robes. One was seated at the head and the other at the foot of the place where Jesus' body had lain. "Woman," they asked her, "why are you weeping?" She answered them, "Because the Lord has been taken away, and I do not know where they have put him." She had no sooner said this than she turned around and caught sight of Jesus standing there.[3] But she did not know him. "Woman," he asked her, "Why are you weeping? Who is it you are looking for?" [(John 20:1 and 11-15, NAB.) Soft music is played as the reader fades away. The storyteller enters sobbing and talks with the pain and confusion of one overcome by grief.]

**Storyteller:** "I just have to be near him one more time and tell him 'Good-bye.'"[4] [She pauses as if listening.] "You wonder what a woman is doing here before daylight? After all I have gone through, the usual fears are nothing." [She has stopped sobbing, but she enters deeply into the emotions of her past.]

"You see I had been so sick—my mind was confused. People said that I was possessed by seven demons. And sometimes my whole body revealed the anguish of my mind.[5] I had heard of this wandering rabbi called Jesus. They said he told stories about the reign of God and cured people. I had little faith or hope in another rabbi. What use is someone who speaks of God? In my depression, I cursed the God who made me as I was. But the women of our town of Magdala were going to sit on the hillside that afternoon and listen to him, so I went. Perhaps someone had told him how often I was out of my mind, or did he just look at my troubled face and know? He came over and knelt down beside me. I began to tremble with fear— what did he want? Some people hated me in my illness. No one seemed to understand the kind of demons that can plague a woman. I think they are different from men's demons.[6] Other people made fun of me and said, 'Crazy woman.' Did this wandering rabbi want to taunt me also? But he looked in my eyes and he called me by name. He knew my name. He said, 'Mary, Mary, be free of your demons.' He looked at me with so much love. Could I love myself as he was loving me? Could I trust myself as he was trusting me? 'You are precious. You are whole,' he said.

"His look of love changed everything for me. I was whole—though often the demons of fear, of self-doubt, of anxiety came back to knock at my door. But now I knew they did not have to stay with me. I, as many other women who were cured, left my home and followed him. We used our money to care for him and his friends. My family didn't understand. Many families didn't.[7] Men could wander around with a traveling rabbi, men could spend their time learning and speaking of the reign of God, but women should stay home.[8] But Jesus would not say that, he never told us to go home and be quiet.

"When that woman in Samaria at the well learned who he was and went to tell everyone about him, the men with Jesus were upset but Jesus was not." [She pauses as if hearing the listener speak.] "Oh.... you say you've heard about me?" [She pauses again.] "You've heard I was like that woman of Samaria—five husbands, maybe more, not a decent woman? No, that is not I. There was a woman who anointed Jesus at the house of Simon, the Pharisee. Jesus looked with love and forgiveness at that woman. Some say that she had known many men, but I am not that woman. Perhaps the friends of Peter confused our stories. They have been jealous because Jesus has shared so much with me. Now that Peter left him and I stayed, I do not know what they will say."[9] [She pauses and looks away.]

"But I want to tell you about the last night Jesus was with us. We had served the supper, and a few of us were cleaning up afterward. Jesus took some of his friends and went to the garden where he liked to pray. Martha and I told him we'd come later. We were nearby praying when we heard shouting.[10] A group of people came and arrested Jesus. We followed trying to see him. All night we tried to get near as they took him to Caiaphas' house, as they tormented him, as they took him to Pilate, and as they scourged him. Who would have believed that these people who had said, 'Hosanna to the Son of David. Blessed is he who comes in the name of the Lord'—that these same people would shout, 'Crucify him. We have no king but Caesar.' Are they afraid to let God rule their lives?

"The disciple Jesus loved, his mother Mary, and I stood at his cross. Why did I stay in such pain? Maybe I should have run away like Peter and Andrew and Thomas—but I could not. Like women in labor pains, Mary and I did not try to escape the pain. Like our mothers who care for the dying we would not leave. We are acquainted with sorrow, familiar with grief. We bear the iniquities of many. We stayed until the end, and then we hurried to bury him before the Sabbath. We hardly had any time. Now, I need to finish that. One needs time to grieve, time to say good-bye."

[She puts her hands over her face and quietly starts to sob again. In this next section, she must clearly visualize the tomb, the angels, and the Christ, and relate to each with such conviction that the people too can visualize them. She walks over, stoops down and looks in the tomb. She looks around and not finding Christ's body, she starts to sob again. She hears the angels' question.]

**Storyteller:** "You want to know why I am weeping?[11] Because the Lord has been taken away, and I do not know where they have put him." [She turns and walks a few steps away. Her head is down and she is wiping away tears. She slightly notices someone else there, but she does not really look at the person.] "Why am I weeping? Whom do I seek?"[12] [She pauses.] "Sir, if you are the one who carried him off, tell me where you have laid him." [She continues to sob, then suddenly her face begins to show joy and amazement.] "Mary, Mary? You know my name?[13] Rabboni!" [She steps forward, goes down on one knee, and clasps as if she were holding him. The next section should be played humorously. Resurrection is the greatest comedy of all.]

"You do not want me to cling to you?[14] Well, if I don't, you might just slip away again. I thought you were dead and gone." [She pauses and listens.] "You have not yet ascended to the Father? You want me to go to your brothers and sisters and tell them that you are alive? That you are ascending to your Father who is our Father? Your God who is our God?" [She puts her hands on her hips and is feisty and funny.] "Jesus, you have always said the silliest things, 'Happy are the poor.... Happy are those who mourn.... Happy are you when they persecute you!' And now you are saying this!" [She listens again.] "You are sending *me* to tell your brothers that you are alive?

"I can't go. I am not the one to speak. Who would believe a woman? Who would believe one who has been ill? Who would believe one who hasn't studied?" [She might improvise and add comments like, "To speak for you, someone has to have a degree. They have to be straight. They couldn't be elderly. They have to have been ordained. They have to be smart. They couldn't be handicapped."] "The men would never accept me teaching them." [She listens but still looks confused.] "They will believe me because I *resemble you*?"

(If this is done for Roman Catholics familiar with the Vatican document that women cannot be ordained because they do not physically resemble Jesus, she can look down at her female body, slightly touch her breast and say, "Jesus, we all know I do not resemble you; the pope says I do not resemble you." After people have finished laughing, she changes the mood. This moves from comedy to a poignant recognition of woundedness. She speaks slowly and seriously.)

"How do I resemble you?"

(The next lines can be spoken, but it has usually been more effective to do this in mime challenging the listeners to answer the question within themselves.)

### Spoken option

"Yes, I do know the wounds in my feet and my hands." [She pauses.] "Yes, I too have a wound in my heart." [She holds out her hands in a gesture of crucifixion.]

### Mime option

(The music of the chant "My God, my all, Jesus, Jesus," from *Chants for Meditation*, by Rufino Zaragoza, O.F.M. Conv. [*National Catholic Reporter*, P. O. Box 281, Kansas City, MI 64141], is played softly. The storyteller turns her back and takes some red clown makeup or lipstick which can be on the table or in her pocket. She marks large "wounds" in each of her hands. In slow dance-mime movements she stretches out her arms in a gesture of crucifixion then she turns around. The chant grows louder. She can simply hold that position for a few moments or move into a dance expressing pain and anguish, but finally quiet strength.

After the mime or the words, there are two ways to invite the listeners' participation.)

### Anointing option

(The storyteller and some of the other ministers gently anoint each other's palms with red dots or "wounds" and then they begin passing the makeup among the people so that all may do this. The chant continues during this.)

### Sharing option

(The storyteller says, "Thomas knew that the living person before him was really the One who had died by the wounds he saw and felt. Mary knew that resurrected life was possible in the midst of death because she knew wounds, pains, and difficulties in her life. You are invited to turn to a partner, touch each other's hands, touch each other's wounds. For a few moments share how you might know woundedness in your life or in the world today, and then how you know resurrection." The music can be played softly as people talk.

Then she continues, "Let us remember that we who know the wounds of Jesus can also know the healing, peace, and joy of the risen Christ. Let us share with each other a greeting of peace." People do this in a customary way.)

**Storyteller:** "I have seen the Lord. And if you doubt this story—if you doubt that there may be life in the midst of death—you may touch my wounds. *I have seen the Lord.* And in his leap of resurrection he teaches us to dance 'Alleluias.' Let us stand and dance and sing." [Any joyful acclamation or refrain with "Alleluia" may be sung, and the storyteller leads people raising and lowering alternate arms, swaying back and forth, or dancing in a circle. At the end of this, bread and wine are brought to the table. Though this is not necessary, "canopies" of crepe paper can be carried over them and placed on each side of the table. These can be seen in the photographs.]

**Second Clown:** "Let us gather around the table and join in prayer." [Pause]

"We praise you, Loving God, as we celebrate that great surprise of death transformed into life.

"What we considered the end is the beginning.

"What the world considered foolish is a manifestation of your great wisdom.

Illustration 14: The bread and wine are brought to the table.

"So we gather with holy men and women through the ages and join in dance and song:"

[All sing a joyful acclamation such as "Alleluia," or "Mary Magdelene's Song," by Colleen Fulmer, which may be found in the Appendix. The clowns lead in a gesture of raising the right arm on the first line, the left arm on the second line, both arms down on the third, and then a powerful movement of both arms up with hands bursting open on the last.]

**First Clown:** "We thank you, God, that from the very beginning you called woman and man to be in partnership and to reflect different aspects of your image.

"We image you as sisters, as fathers, as clowns, as friends, as brothers, as lovers, as mothers, as shepherds, as seamstresses, as dreamers, as dancers, as fools, as servants.

"We thank you for our parents in faith, Abraham and Sarah, whom you blessed with a child called 'Isaac,' that is 'laughter,' when they knew sorrow.

"We remember Moses who led your people from bondage to freedom, and Miriam who led your freed people in dance and song.

"We too have been freed so we join in dance and song:"

[All do the acclamation.]

**Storyteller:** "Through the ages, you have continued to bless your people with all good gifts and to teach them to laugh and to dance.

"We remember your greatest gift, Jesus, one full of the greatest wisdom and the greatest folly.

"He put a little child as the greatest.

"He called the poor, the persecuted, and those who mourn, blessed.

"He strengthened all who mourn by assuring Mary Magdalene who stood near him in death that she could be a witness to his resurrection.

"He brought healing to all who deny and doubt when he assured Peter who denied him and Thomas who doubted him that they could know forgiveness."

**Second Clown:** "Loving Creator, pour out upon us the Spirit of the Risen Christ, that we may dance though we are in bondage, that we may laugh though we face death, that we may bring the healing, forgiveness, and peace that the risen Savior gives us to the ends of the earth.

Illustration 15: Pour out upon us the Spirit of the Risen Christ that we may dance though we are in bondage

"Let us join in dance and song:"

[All do the acclamation.]

**First Clown:** "Let us hold hands as one family of God around this table and pray to God, who is like a mother and a father to us." [All say or sing the "Our Father." Then, she raises the bread for all to see.]

**Second:** "'Jesus knew that the hour had come for him to pass from this world....He got up from table, removed his outer garment and taking a towel began to wash the feet of his disciples.'

"For a moment, he remembered how good it felt when his mother had washed his little feet and cuddled him close.

"He remembered when the woman had poured her warm, salty tears over his tired feet, soothing salt water healing his weariness, healing her hurt.

"He remembered Mary, Martha's sister, who massaged his feet with sweet ointment—more sweetness and gentleness than a hard, practical world could take.

"Jesus, touched by women, gentle and strong enough to touch others with your wounded hands, touch us now.

"'While they were at table, Jesus took the bread and broke it.' For a moment he remembered watching his mother knead, bake, break, and share bread, again and again and again." [The first clown starts to break the bread in pieces.]

**Second Clown:** "He remembered Peter's mother-in-law, who rose from her sickness to serve him bread.

"He remembered, 'They gave a banquet for Jesus and Martha served.'

"Martha served so much that he invited her to rest, to sit and talk. 'Jesus loved Martha.'

"Martha invited him to talk less and serve more.

"And so, he made bread of his own body.

"He took the bread, blessed it, and broke it.

"'And near the cross of Jesus stood his mother and his mother's sister, Mary the wife of Clopas, and Mary of Magdala.'

"They saw, they began to understand the breaking of the bread.

"Jesus, with your wounded hands, teach us how to break bread."

**Storyteller:** "Let us share this bread and wine and remember him." [They begin to pass these. The song "We Are the Body of Christ," which may be found in the Appendix, is sung. People may be seated; after all are finished, there should be a brief silence.]

**First Clown:** A meditation from Paul's second letter to the Corinthians:

"My grace is enough for you.... (II Cor. 12:9-10 is read).

Illustration 16: May we, like Mary, go forth and proclaim that Christ is alive

**Second Clown:** "Let us rise and pray." [Pause] "Gracious God, we, your foolish people, thank you for this mystery of death made life, of sorrow transformed into joy. May we, like Mary Magdalene, go forth and proclaim that Christ is alive. This we pray in his name. Amen."

[A traditional Easter hymn may be sung, or "Ruah" or "Passionate Life," by Colleen Fulmer, which may be found in the Appendix.]

## For Further Reflection, Journalizing, and /or Discussion

Scriptural Background: John 20:11-18, Mark 16:9-11, and Luke 8:1-3

1. Have you ever been so caught up in worry or grief that you could not recognize the risen Christ beside you?

2. Do we ever want to stay clinging to the Christ when he is urging us to go out, tell his brothers and sisters that he is risen, and witness to his resurrected life through our living?

3. Some of the first- and second-century writings about Jesus speak of Peter being jealous of Mary of Magdala because Jesus revealed so much to her. How can we learn to value others relationships and gifts without jealousy?

4. Mary recognized Christ's voice when he called her by name. How are names a part of our identity? Does it make me feel good when people know my name and call me by name? Does failing to use people's own name (e.g., serving people being called only "waiter" or "maid," minority people in history books, women after they are married) devalue those people and decrease their self-esteem?

5. Mary describes her demons as fear, self-doubt, and anxiety. How can each of us learn to identify our own demons and learn not to project our demons onto others?

6. How can wounds be the very things that help us to recognize the presence of the risen Christ in ourselves, in others, and in situations in the world? When we admit our vulnerability, we are letting others "touch our wounds." When can this be helpful for ourselves? For others?

7. The Church calls Mary "*apostola apostolorum*," the apostle to the apostles, and in the past, on her feast day, as on the feasts of the other apostles, the Creed, the statement of belief in the risen Christ, was professed. How can women today follow Mary in being apostles to the male apostles?

8. How is staying with the dying, as Mary of Magdala, Jesus' mother, his mother's sister, Mary the wife of Clopas, and John stayed with Jesus on the cross, sharing in "labor pains" of a new life, a new creation?

9. Mary of Magdala has been confused with a woman who was a sinner (Luke 7:36-50). Why do stories of something bad seem to be spread more than stories of something good?

### Readings

• Women to whom Christ revealed himself:

• The Samaritan woman encounters Him and evangelizes her town (John 4:7-42)

• Martha knows Him as the Messiah (John 11:27) as Peter does (Matt. 16:16)

## Reflections on the Development and Use of the Service

When this service was first used at a cluster of theological schools, I had anticipated that it might be particularly meaningful for women since Mary was commissioned as an apostle to the male apostles. What I had not anticipated was the great significance the service had for gay men who identified with her expressing her woundedness. Homosexuality continues to be a sensitive area in relation to those called to ordination. Members of Dignity, the Catholic organization for homosexuals and their friends, invited me to share the story there and to model lay leadership of prayer from a women's perspective. Those who are marginalized can empower others who are, as well.

The service was done at a therapy center for priests, brothers, and sisters who have had emotional problems. In making the choice to come for help, they were showing their wounds, and they deeply entered into Magdalene's recognition.

Many studies have noted that the gospels give no evidence of Mary being a sinner or a prostitute. Early writings speak of Peter's jealousy toward Mary since she was so close to Jesus. The patriarchal church through the ages has extensively developed stories on Mary as a "great sinner" and in doing so detracted from her place as "apostle to the apostles," the ones who had left Jesus.

# Chapter 10

# Martha, Who Served a Banquet for Jesus

## Themes

- Hosting Jesus and his followers in one's home
- Being freed to study and pray instead of being confined to domestic tasks
- Jesus being free enough to join in women's tasks
- Women hosting the early Christian communities' prayer and sacred meals
- Sharing hospitality with all the family of God especially the poor and the needy as a type of eucharistic sharing

## Possible Uses

- Thanksgiving; Easter or Pentecost season; Feast of St. Martha (July 29), or other holy women's feasts
- With lectionary reading on the sixteenth Sunday of Ordinary Time, Cycle C; Tuesday of the twenty-seventh week of the Church Year; with the *Inclusive Language Lectionary*, alternative reading for the second Sunday of Epiphany, Cycle B
- Before any special meal; family or parish celebration; retreat dinner
- Preparation for eucharistic ministry; to relate feeding the hungry to Eucharist

## The Service

(The central core of this service is inviting people's stories, Martha's story, sharing bread, wine, and a meal, then a circle dance. The other prayers and actions have varied considering the time and needs of the groups which have ranged from twenty to two hundred people. In one group, each individual mixed-in an ingredient for cornbread for dinner as the person shared a memory of a meal. It had baked by the end of the prayers. Hostesses can prepare a meal, but inviting all to bring food to share or vegetables to put in a pot of soup is good. The invitations may say, "The early Christians would gather to remember Christ by sharing a meal to which each contributed. You are invited to bring food to our potluck supper where we shall remember their celebrations." Tables should be beautifully set with cloths, flowers, candles, wine glasses, a loaf of bread in a basket, and a bottle of wine and/or grape juice. Round tables of six or eight are desirable. The food is served after the stories and prayer. If the foot-washing or hand-washing is to be used, basins and towels for these should be nearby, but not on the tables. People should be able to turn their chairs to see the storyteller. If there is a very large group, she might stand near a specially decorated and easily visible table as she tells the story. For instance, this has been done at Thanksgiving with an autumn decor.)

**First Reader:** Meals can be special times—Thanksgiving dinners, birthday celebrations, meetings with special friends, or quiet times with family. We as women nourish life in our own bodies and throughout history have spent much of our time and energy feeding and caring for others. Close your eyes for a moment and think of one meal that has been really special for you and why it was special. (Pause for a few moments.) Now open your eyes and let us briefly share a little about these special meals.

(If the groups are very large, the sharing could be done in pairs instead of with the whole group. After a few minutes, the storyteller speaks loudly or makes some noise to interrupt. She is bold and fun-loving.)

**Storyteller:** "You have all been telling stories about special meals. I want to tell you about one of the special meals at our home. You may have heard part of the story, but I want to tell you the *whole story*." [She may pick up a Bible and read or tell this part.] "People tell this much—'On their journey, Jesus entered a village where a woman named Martha welcomed him to her home'—that's me." [She points to herself.] "'She had a sister named Mary, who seated herself at the Lord's feet and listened to his words. Martha, who was busy with all the details of hospitality, came to him and said, 'Lord, are you not concerned that my sister has left me to do the household tasks all alone? Tell her to help me.' The Lord in reply said to her: 'Martha, Martha, you are anxious and upset about many things; one thing only is required. Mary has chosen the better portion and she shall not be deprived of it'" [Luke 10:38-42, NAB].[1]

"Our people tell this story of Jesus on a journey, on the way to Jerusalem, the place of shalom, of peace, of fullness, of harmony, the place of God's reign. People tell this story about a meal along the journey, along the way, so that our growing community who follows Christ may learn more about his way.[2] I had thought that my place was in the kitchen and that Mary's was, too. I'd heard Rabbi Eliezer's advice to the men, 'Rather should the words of the Torah be burned than entrusted to a woman.'[3] I'd seen the men study and discuss the scripture with a rabbi, 'sit at his feet' as they explained it, but I never dared do that.[4] I'd heard the prayer that our brother, Lazarus, was taught to say, 'Thank you God that you did not make me a Gentile. Thank you God that you did not make me a woman. Thank you God that you did not make me ignorant.'[5] As much as I hungered to savor, to discuss, to share the scriptures, I didn't dare to sit at the feet of a rabbi and do that—women can't do things like that. There are meals to be prepared, clothes to be made, washing to be done.

"But that day, the one I was telling you about, Jesus freed me from all that. He freed me by sharing the burden." [This should be exaggerated and humorous.] "I listened to him—I didn't have to make five kinds of fancy foods to please him. He said only one thing was necessary. You probably haven't heard what I said to Jesus after that." [She shakes her finger or gestures vehemently as she speaks.] "I told Him, 'Well, maybe only one is necessary, but if I sit here like You and Mary, there won't even be one thing for supper. There will be *no supper at all.*[6] I know lots of people who know how to talk, but Jesus knew how to listen. He got up and went into the kitchen and finished peeling and slicing the onions that I'd started. Mary followed Him, and the three of us could talk both about the price of figs this season and the pearl of great price. We could talk of the leaven in the dough we kneaded and the reign of God being like leaven. When he came to share in the work, I no longer needed to be anxious and upset about many things. Jesus understood my complaint. When some people expect others to bear the burden of labor, to provide food, to provide all the basic needs while they have the leisure to sit and discuss, to enjoy the good life, how can they criticize those of us who labor for being anxious and upset?

"When Jesus was gone—well, when the officials thought they'd gotten rid of this revolutionary—Mary and I continued to have special meals at our house. We're sisters who have learned to share our different gifts and our hospitality. With our friends, we would share the stories of Jesus. I shall never forget our grief when our brother Lazarus died, but finally Jesus came. Though my anger and hurt were great, in the very midst of them I knew Jesus was the Messiah.[7] His love and life were stronger than any bonds of death. We remembered the banquet for Jesus at which I served the week before he died.[8] Jesus loved Mary, our brother and me very much—and he loved to come for our cooking.

"As I was saying, after his death, when the community gathered at our house, we sang psalms. We read the scriptures to our brothers and sisters. Mary and I shared the stories of Jesus' meals at our home." [She raises the bread.] "We baked, blessed, and broke bread and gave thanks—and He wasn't gone, He was there among us, just as truly as that day when He said, 'Martha, Martha....'[9]

"Having special meals really wasn't anything new. Momma had done it, Grandmother had done it." [She points out the decorations as she speaks of them.] "Every Sabbath eve they prepared special foods, and on the Passover, that most sacred of nights, they lit the candles and began the beautiful prayers. On Sukkoth, the feast of the harvest, the feast of thanksgiving, they decorated with fruit and leaves and praised God for the bounty of creation. No, having special meals wasn't anything new, yet Jesus had started a new thing. Before, people had looked to the rabbis and the priests for leadership." [She points to all there.] "Now, the Spirit was poured out on all people, 'Old men dreamed dreams, young men saw visions, daughters prophesied.' The daughters of Philip were prophesying and teaching in Caesarea. Many women are prophesying in Corinth.[10] Women all over were gathering churches in their homes.[11] When Peter was arrested, the believers were afraid, but Mary, the mother of Mark, gathered them at her house for prayer and the breaking of bread as she always did. Their prayers were so powerful, Peter's chains broke and he knew he should go to her house to thank her. We heard of the church in Colossia that meets at Nympha's house. Paul just couldn't thank and praise Lydia enough. She was one of the best merchants in Philippi and she was just as good selling Christianity to her people as she was selling purple dye. Other women of her town, Euodia and Syntyche, labored side by side with Paul in teaching the gospel in that area.[12]

"But I don't need to go on telling you about the leaders of the house churches, the women who made bread, broke it, and taught the family of believers to give thanks.[13] You know the stories of opening one's home to feed the hungry, because in Christ's church, the hungry are our own family. You know stories of these women—of Priscilla, of Apphia, of Phoebe,[14] of Junia, of Chloe—I need to write Chloe and the church that gathers at her house a letter. She, like Paul, has been upset about some of the believers in Corinth.

"When they gather for meals they are not noticing the needy and the weak in their midst. Everyone is in such a hurry to start his or her own supper that one goes hungry while another is getting drunk. The poor are being embarrassed. Some groups are making divisions. They are even putting Jew over Gentile, free over slave, and male over female. If they do this, they cannot call the bread they break Christ's supper .[15]

"I know Jesus who helped me slice the onions that day, Jesus who invited me to study scripture with Him, wouldn't allow such divisions. Yes, I must write Chloe about that day when Jesus was helping me in the kitchen."[16] [She is seated and there is a silent pause or soft music.]

**Second Reader:** We recall the celebrations of the Sabbath in Jewish homes. Through the centuries, Jewish women have begun the ritual, saying the prayers as they light the candles. Let us close our eyes as darkness comes.

(The lights are turned down. Soft instrumental music is played in the background.)

**First:** Let us open our eyes and light the festal lights. Blessed are you, loving God who brings light to our eye and joy to our hearts. (The candles are lit.)

**Second:** Creator God, you have given us the splendors of creation, a reflection of your glory. You give beauty and food for all your family. Though again and again we turned from you, you have raised up wise women to challenge, give courage, and lead. We remember Deborah, the prophetess, who ruled your people wisely and stood firm protecting your people, when men were afraid.

We remember Miriam, the prophetess and leader of worship; she brought your daughters from bondage to freedom and led song and dance claiming freedom, giving you praise.

**First:** We remember Abigail, wise, peace-loving woman, who brought food for the hungry to mediate between two proud men who were ready to turn to violence.

We remember Huldah, the prophetess who had revelations for priests, elders, and king—Huldah who brought your words to challenge a corrupt nation.

We remember Esther, blessed with wealth and prestige, who risked her position and her life to save the lives of your people.

We remember Ruth and Naomi, women left without men, who cared for and comforted each other imaging you in their sisterly faithfulness.

**Storyteller:** "At our tables, let us mention aloud or in the depths of our hearts the names of others, past and present, whom we remember." [Pause for people to mention names.]

"With those we have mentioned and with all your angels and saints, we gather around this table to praise you and give you thanks.

"At our tables, let us each share a word or a phrase of what bread means to us." [Pause for people to do this.] "Let us each share what wine means to us." [Pause for people to do this.] "Let us stand and stretch forth our hands in blessing over these gifts." [Pause for this.] "Sisters, we feed most of the people of the world. Let us feed each other this holy meal. Let us break and share this bread, remembering our sisters Martha and Mary who hosted Jesus. Let us share this wine remembering him."

(As these are shared, the chant "Martha's Profession of Faith," by Colleen Fulmer and Rufino Zaragoza, O.F.M. Conv., or "We Are the Body of Christ," by Martha Ann Kirk and Colleen Fulmer, which can be found in the Appendix, is sung.)

**Second:** All of our meals are sacred times. Let us continue our prayer through conversation, laughter, and storytelling. Let us share food brought by all of us, a "multiplication of loaves and fishes."

(The meal is served. When all are finished, people are invited to listen. The first reader raises a Bible and reads John 12:1-4.)

**First:** A reading from the Gospel According to John.

"Six days before Passover...

**Second:** The gospel goes on to say that a week later at another special meal with beloved friends, Jesus did something like what Mary had done for him. (She takes the Bible and reads John 13:1,4-8a.)

"Before the feast of Passover...

(She puts down the gospel and pauses.) Peter was upset. Footwashing was something servants did for masters. The Talmud says that wives should wash their husbands feet, hands, and face even if they had servants.[17] Jesus was acting like a wife. Peter seems to have understood this, because when Jesus objected, Peter responded to also wash his hands and face. Jesus confused and dismantled the systems of hierarchy; he challenged all who would have "power over" rather than "power with." Jesus challenged all who would stay at a distance from others, never touching or letting themselves be touched. Let us pray that we may pour out our love as freely as Mary poured her ointment, though Judas objected. Let us pray that we may dismantle systems of hierarchy as boldly as Jesus who washed feet, though Peter objected.

(There are two options for symbolic action.)

### First Option

**First:** Let someone from each table wash the feet (or hands) of the person next to him or her. Then, let that person do the same for the next, until we have all been washed. (Soft music is played as this is done.)

### Second Option

**First:** Again and again, scripture speaks of God's healing and God's grace coming through touch. Our world has much violent physical contact. The women of the world have often been touched violently. Let us touch each other with reverence and gentleness praying that all in the world may know God's healing touch. Let us find a partner and spend some time giving each other a foot (or a hand) massage. (Soft music is played as this is done.)

**Storyteller:** "Let us rise and place our chairs so we can stand in a large circle around the room" [or, if this is impossible, in circles around the tables].

"The *Acts of John*, an early text, describes Jesus and his friends singing and doing a circle dance at the Last Supper.[18] Maybe they did; Jewish celebrations often had folk dance. Or maybe the text reflects the dances that the early Christians did when they gathered for Eucharist. Dances used in the first few centuries of Christianity were discouraged, as clergy began to separate from and put themselves above the rest of the Christian community. Circle dancing affirms unity and equal dignity. Let us reclaim the circle dance of a discipleship of equals. Let us hold hands and dance. Follow my gestures for the chorus and circle to the right on the verses."

(If the dance is done at each table, a person from each could learn it ahead of time or it could be practiced with the group. "We Are the Body of Christ" or "Ruah," which may be found in the Appendix, are sung and danced.)

**Second:** Graced by each other's stories, nourished by this holy meal, let us go forth to share our gifts.

## For Further Reflection, Journalizing, and/or Discussion

Scriptural Background: Luke 10:38-42; I Cor. 11:17-34; and John 11:1-44 and 12:1-11

### Questions

1. Are we doubtful of or critical of the ways others freely relate to Christ or witness to him? Do we allow others and ourselves time to sit at the feet of Christ and learn from him?

2. Women who have sat at "the feet of Christ"—that is, been his disciples—and to whom Christ has revealed himself, have responsibility to shepherd and feed the flock of Christ. How are women carrying out this responsibility?

3. The story of Martha was a reminder to women who hosted eucharistic gatherings of the early Church in their homes to focus on Christ's presence and not worry about the material concerns. How can we learn to be more present to Christ in each other in all our meals?

4. Paul praises Phoebe, the woman deacon of the church of Cenchreae (Rom. 16:1). Recommendations for women deacons are given in I Tim. 3:11. The fourth-century Apostolic Constitutions gives the text for the ordination of women deacons, and many other early church writings speak of them. What would be the advantages and disadvantages of reviving the ordination and ministry of women deacons?

5. How is the home still the basic unit of the Church? How do house churches, that is, people meeting in smaller groups, bring enrichment to the larger assemblies of the Church?

6. The body of Christ is not just the historical Jesus symbolized by the bread and the wine; the body of Christ is all the community. When people share the supper, but do not recognize Christ's body, they are calling judgment upon themselves. In what ways are we calling judgment upon ourselves when we greedily use the goods of the world and fail to recognize the poor and those in need as Christ's body?

7. Prophets or prophetesses convey both challenges and consolation. Telling women's stories can be a prophetic task. What challenges and what consolations have we experienced through reflection on these scripture stories?

### Readings

Women who freely relate to Christ while others object or refuse to believe them

• Woman at Simon the Pharisee's house (Luke 7:36-50)

• Woman at Simon the leper's house (Mark 14:3-8; and Matt. 26:6-13)

• Mary of Bethany (John 12:3-8)

• The Samaritan woman at the well (John 4:4-42)

• Women who encounter the risen Christ (Mark 16:11; and Luke 24:11)

Women leaders of the early Christian communities

• Mary, the mother of John Mark (Acts 12:12)

• Priscilla (Acts 18:1-3, 18-19 and 24-26; Rom. 16:3-5; and II Tim. 4:19)

- Lydia (Acts 16:14-15, 40)

- Nympha (Col. 4:15)

- Chloe (I Cor.1:11)

- Junia, an "outstanding apostle" (Rom. 16:7)

- Apphia (Philem. 1-2)

- Euodia and Syntyche (Phil. 4:2-3)

- Four prophetesses, daughters of Philip (Acts 21:9)

- No more distinctions between classes, sexes, and races (Gal. 3:28)

## Reflections on the Development and Use of the Service

Despite the attitudes of many of us that we have a thoroughly incarnational Christology, and a liberated vision beyond imaging who should and should not do domestic tasks, Jesus in the kitchen slicing the onions always gets howls of laughter. In my early presentations, I had a soft-spoken Martha, but the more carefully I read the biblical texts the more I felt that she was a strong and assertive woman. Yet, she did not seem brusque; she seemed to have a humorous and affectionate strength.

A sharing of this story led to invitations to learn from and share with New Catholic Horizons, a basic Christian community that has gathered for "house church" every week for several years. Their joys and their struggles gave me insight into what joys and struggles the "house churches" of early Christianity may have had. Their spirituality and wisdom have enriched many parts of this project. At this time, over half of the Roman Catholics in the world do not have priests available to celebrate Sunday Eucharist. Clergy compose less than one-half of 1 percent of the Catholic population. Seventy percent of the parishes in France do not have priests. Over 770 parishes in the United States do not. The numbers of priestless parishes in Third World countries is even greater. The story of Martha has proven to be very significant for many who are forming basic Christian communities.

Both the sharing of stories about significant meals and the sharing of a meal in this service has been enjoyed. Even without religious allusions, a meal with friends seems to be one of the most meaningful human experiences. Our God is one who chose to come not through theophany, but through what is most human. Our eyes continue to be opened in the breaking of bread.

Illustration 17: Let us reclaim the circle dance of a discipleship of equal.

# Chapter 11

# With Dorcas Let Us Sew a Garment of Love to Cover Our World

## Themes

• Clothing the needy

• Performing other works of mercy

• Valuing those who care for people's needs

• God who clothes the world

• Creating beauty to sustain people

• Remembering resurrects those who have died

## Possible Uses

• Easter season, All Saints' Day, feasts of holy women who did works of mercy

• The Third Week of Easter

• Programs on caring for the needy, women's history, solidarity with Third World women and other workers; programs for those who sew and do fiber arts and crafts

## The Service

(All participants are invited to bring garments or pieces of sewing, weaving, knitting, quilting, baby clothes, sewn dolls or animals, etc., that are special to them. Perhaps they made these; perhaps the pieces are keepsakes in their families. Perhaps they are beautiful things created by our sisters in other parts of the world. People are also invited to bring clothes for the needy which will be collected at the end of the service. As people arrive, the room is decorated with what they bring, both in an arrangement in the middle of the circle and hanging on the walls around. Chairs are in a circle and a table in the middle has an arrangement of needles, thread, cloth, and a Bible. The Bible might have an attractive stitchery cover. On each chair there is a strip of material [about two or three inches by two or three feet] for each of the participants. Some should have thread, needles and scissors which can be shared. The atmosphere should feel like both a "sewing circle" and a worship service. The reader/ministers should speak loudly to be heard, but should stay in their places around the circle except for the reading from Acts.)

**First Reader:** Let us be quiet and breathe deeply for awhile. In silence, let us be aware of the Spirit speaking through all of us and through our sisters through the ages. (Silence for a few minutes.)

**Second Reader:** When the day of Pentecost.... (Acts 2:1-4 is read.)

**Third Reader:** Your sons and *daughters*.... (Acts 2:36-42 is read.)

**Fourth Reader:** Daughters and handmaids were filled with the Spirit, but then the Acts of the Apostles continues to tell stories of Peter and John, of Paul and Mark, of James and Barnabas, of Stephen and Philip— yet we know the women too witnessed to the Christ. We have little pieces of the stories of the women, such as Mary the mother of John Mark who hosted believers in her home, Lydia who gathered people for prayer in Philippi, Priscilla who taught Apollos, and Tabitha called Dorcas, a beloved leader in Joppa. Legend says that Dorcas made clothes for orphans and the needy. Perhaps she was a leader of a group of widows. Let us listen to her story.

**Fifth Reader:** (She goes forward and takes the Bible from the table and reads Acts 9:36-42.)

A reading from the Acts of the Apostles.

"Now in Joppa...."[1]

This is the word of God. (She returns the Bible to the table and is seated, and there is a moment of silence.)

**First:** Not everyone who says, "Lord, Lord," shall enter the reign of heaven.

**Second:** And who shall enter heaven?

**Third:** Jesus said, "Inherit the reign...." (Matt. 25:34b-36 is read).

**Fourth:** Dorcas' "life was marked by constant good deeds and acts of charity."

(The following are like an echo.)

**Fifth:** Dorcas' "life was marked by constant good deeds and acts of charity."

**First:** Dorcas' "life was marked by constant good deeds and acts of charity."

**Second:** Our sisters through the ages have performed the works of mercy, fed the hungry, clothed the naked, visited the imprisoned, sheltered the homeless—yet where are their names? Who sings their praises? We remember the names of Peter and Paul who spoke, we forget the names of their sisters who silently did the deeds on which Christ says we will be judged.

**Third:** Our sisters who clothed so many with Christ's warm love, are cold in death, dead and cold in being forgotten, uncelebrated. God hears our cries today; God says, women arise.

**Fourth:** We women, like Dorcas, sit right up and the good works go on! Now let's stand right up and sing of our God and of women through the ages.

(All sing "Dorcas' Song," by Martha Ann Kirk and Colleen Fulmer, which can be found in the Appendix.)

(People around the room speak as they point to the sewing near them or that they are wearing. These are comments about things we had. With a little effort of checking labels and asking questions, it is not difficult to find garments from many parts of the world.)

**Participant 1:** Let us not forget our sisters who see that our sheets are woven in the mills of the Carolinas.

**Participant 2:** Let us not forget our sisters who sew our shoes in the factories of the Philippines.

**Participant 3:** Let us not forget our aunts who created dolls for the children that we love.

**Participant 4:** Let us not forget our sisters who embroidered flowers on our dresses in the homes of Mexico.

**Participant 5:** Let us not forget our sisters who batiked our skirts in the huts of Java.

**Participant 6:** Let us not forget our grandmothers who quilted our covers putting love in each stitch.

**Participant 7:** Let us not forget our sisters who wove our belts on their little looms in Guatemala.

**Participant 8:** Let us not forget our sisters who made our coats in the factories of Hong Kong.

**Participant 9:** Let us not forget our friends who knitted our mufflers to warm our hearts as well as our necks.

**Participant 10:** Let us not forget our sisters who are sewing the stories of their oppression on *arpilleras* in violence-torn parts of South America.[2]

**Participant 11:** Let us not forget when we buy this handwoven African hanging for only twenty dollars that took over forty hours to make. We are both helping and hurting our sister who made it.

**Fifth:** You are invited to show us and tell about the sewing, knitting, or other things that you have brought, or tell us stories of those who made them, or of others who work with textiles.[3]

(People share. Often, stories about sewing are stories about relationships between people or "rites of passage" in people's lives. The storytelling of the group is of central importance in this "sewing circle prayer," but if some outside stimulation is sought, here are some possible starters:

1. Women in early America often gathered and made quilts at times of transition, so-called "rites of passage" (weddings, births, out of the clothes of the deceased as they were mourned).[4] As they did this they shared stories and wisdom. Have you created for someone at a special time or has someone done this for you?

2. Cloth dolls and puppets which women have created have not withstood the ravages of time like the sculptures of the pharaohs, the stone saints of Notre

Dame, or the wooden totems of the Native Americans; yet, women's soft sculptures have brought children joy, security, and taught relationships. Literature on feminist utopias describes the creation of children's toys and games as the most important work of the society because it shapes the future. Marlo Thomas wrote a children's song, "Willie Wants a Doll," about boys needing parenting skills. What are your experiences with dolls?

3. While sewing and creating fiber arts have often been loving acts for women and gestures of relationship, these same skills have been the source of economic exploitation of women. This is an excerpt from Valerie Quinney's article "Textile Women: Three Generations in the Mill":

> The textile industry has traditionally employed great numbers of women, families exist in which mother, daughter and granddaughter have all worked in one area's mills. Martha Simpson, for example, first entered textile mills in Carrboro, North Carolina in 1908, when she was just nine years old. She later moved to another mill town where her daughter Fay, began work in 1930 at age 16. Another 22 years later, in 1952, Fay's daughter Janie, like her mother and grandmother, went into the mills, getting her first job at 18....Janie was married at 16, but when she saw the marriage was a mistake, she went into the mills to earn money for a divorce—before she got pregnant. Fay had not wanted any of her children to work in textiles because "it's dirty work going on, and you always see favoritism....all the bossmen and straw bosses had women down there in the mill belonging to them, and they were the one to get the snap jobs." To Janie, however, there was very little option, given her education, sex and economic background, except going into the mill.[5]

Maria Riley, in discussing multinational corporations, exploitation of women workers, writes that women comprise about 85% of the work force in textile, electronics and garment industries. She is a key bargaining chip governments use to attract corporations to their countries. She is variously described as "cheap," "docile," "nimble-fingered," and "well-fit by nature for monotonous work." However, it is not that young woman's good disposition or physical dexterity that make her an ideal worker, but her strengths are used as an excuse to justify her abuse.[6]

(After time for sharing and discussion, the prayer continues.)

**First:** These sisters are like the God of creation who clothed Adam and Eve.[7] They are like the God of the Exodus who saw that the wandering people in the wilderness did not go without clothes.[8] They are like the God of celebration who clothes the lilies of the field.[9]

**Second:** For a few moments in silence, let us reflect on all who have made the things in this room. Let us reflect on our sisters going back to pre-historic times who have made garments and beautiful things. (Pause.)

**Third:**

Let us celebrate our sisters,
Let us value their work,
Let us pay them well,
Let us reward them with rest.

And let us remember those who cloth the naked shall sit on God's right hand.

**Fourth:** Sisters, let us sew a garment of a new creation. Let us make raiments of warmth and beauty for our cold world. While the Pentagon makes ever bigger plans to divide us, the sisters of Dorcas have sewn a ribbon of peace to unite the human family.

(Many people have participated in sewing designs on the "Peace Ribbon" which was made to circle the Pentagon as a hope and prayer for peace in 4 August 1985.[10] So many people supported the idea that the ribbon turned out to be long enough to encircle the Lincoln Memorial, the Mall, the Washington Monument, and the Ellipse as well. If pictures or descriptions of the "Peace Ribbon" are available, or if anyone in the group helped work on it, news of this could be shared.)

**Fifth:** Yes, while the sisters of Dorcas have sewn a ribbon of peace to unite the human family, the money used for missiles is quilts stolen from freezing old women.

**First:** Let us sew more quilts.

**Second:** The money used for submarines is shoes stolen from girls working in the fields.

**Third:** Let us make more shoes.

**Fourth:** The money used for tanks is shirts stolen from our sick sons.

**Fifth:** Let us sew more shirts.

**All Readers:** We will sew and sew, sew all together in a ribbon of love.

**First:** Let us beat our bombs into baby blankets. Let us makes our missiles into shelters.

**All Readers:** We will sew and sew, sew all together in a ribbon of love.

**Second:** And though differences may rip us apart....

**All Readers:** (Louder.) We will sew and sew, sew all together in a ribbon of love.

**Third:** In solidarity with our sisters through the ages and throughout the world who sew, let us sew these separate pieces at each of our places into one long ribbon, and finally let us sew the ends of the ribbon together to make a circle. Let us sew bonds that are stronger than the barriers which have divided us. Some of you brought clothes for the needy with you. As we sew, let us pray that these people may be covered with peace as well as clothing. Let us wrap them with warm love. You are invited to place these clothes for the needy in the center of the circle in the basket which will be placed there.

(As the sewing is going on "Martha's Profession of Faith," "Passionate God," "We Are the Body of Christ," or "Ruah," found in the Appendix, may be sung softly in the background. After all the pieces are joined, invite everyone to stand on the inside of the ribbon circle with it over their shoulders.)

**Fourth:** Let us pray to the God who has united us. (Pause.) God who clothes the lilies of the field, we thank you that you encircle us with your love and clothe us with your peace. We thank you for sisters like Dorcas who have clothed the needy. May they continue to live as we celebrate and imitate their good deeds. Bless all who will wear the clothes which we have brought; they stand with us in this circle of your family. Bless us that we may mend and join the divisions within in our world. This we pray in Christ's name. Amen.

**Fifth:** As we create in our spinning, weaving, and sewing, we are re-created. Let us go in peace.

As we patch up what is worn, join together what is ripped apart, we are strengthened and made whole. Let us go in peace.

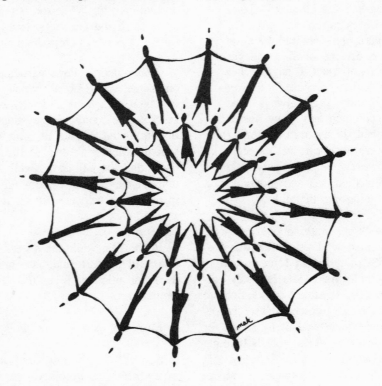

Illustration 18: Let us gather in a circle
by Martha Ann Kirk CCVI

As we clothe those in need, we cover ourselves with a garment that will not wear out. Let us go in peace.

As we see how our God has clothed the earth with such beauty, we learn to create the beautiful. Let us go in peace. In beauty it is finished.

("Washerwoman God," by Martha Ann Kirk and Colleen Fulmer which is found in the Appendix, may be sung and danced.)

# For Further Reflection, Journalizing, and/or Discussion

Scriptural Background: Acts 9:36-43 and Matt. 25:34-36

## Questions

1. Do you sew, knit, quilt, weave, embroider, or do other fiber arts and crafts? Do you find the process one of centering and re-creation?

2. When we buy economical shoes or clothes which have been made in other countries, how are we helping and how are we hurting workers?

3. Churches and groups are starting to promote the sewing and crafts of Third World people in ways that will profit and not exploit the people. How can we support these efforts?

4. Margaret Mead, the anthropologist, noted that in every known society occupations have different value depending on whether men or women practice them. If "such activities are appropriate occupations of men, then the whole society, men and women alike, vote them as important. When the same occupations are performed by women, they are regarded as less important."[11] Why do you think this happens? What can be done?

5. How does teaching history as a story of war and male political rulers, instead of as a story of those who birth, feed, nurture, cloth, and heal people, reinforce war and male political rulers and continue the devaluation of women?

6. Liberation theologians speak of "subversive memory," that is, remembering the oppressed in ways that will strengthen us to overcome oppression today. Whom do you remember?

## Readings

Other women who performed acts of mercy:

• Abigail who fed David and his men (I Sam. 25:1-43)

• Rizpah who buried the dead (II Sam. 21:1-14)

• Shunammite woman who gave food and shelter to Elisha (II Kgs. 4:8-11)

• Wife who feeds and clothes (Prov. 31:10-31)

• Peter's mother-in-law who served as soon as she was cured (Mark 1:29-31)

• Women who helped bury Jesus (Mark 15:47-16:1 and Luke 23:54-56)

# Reflections on the Development and Use of This Service

The environments of these services that have suddenly appeared five minutes before the prayer have surprised and delighted all of us. People have been invited to bring sewing and fiber crafts to display. The praying-sewing rooms have been transformed into a combination of doll and toy shop, international boutique, contemporary fiber arts exhibit, and museum of family heirlooms like quilts. They have been some of the most festive environments that I have experienced for worship, and they have also had a very warm "homey feeling" that comes from shawls knitted by grandmothers and bonnets ready for the new baby.

The dialogue-homily-storytelling has ranged from warm, nostalgic memories of great-aunts who taught needlework, to deep anger about the exploitation of textile workers. A Filipino woman told sad stories of the exploitation of women there as she showed their handiwork. Men attending have said that the world of sewing seems foreign to them. Only one man, who enjoyed doing costumes for dramas, had any experience in these areas. The men lamented that they did not seem to understand or feel the relationships that women seem to have in sewing for family or friends. Though men are tailors and fashion designers, the fact that ordinary men who sew are often made fun of as homosexuals was discussed. Discrimination against women and discrimination against homosexuals seems to be closely related. Sewing, even more than cooking and childcare, seems to be given pejorative connotations as "women's work."

The reflections led into other areas of economic discrimination. One of my priest colleagues in graduate school had a job in my parish. His work was to celebrate one Eucharist a day, which took less than thirty minutes on weekdays, and to hear confessions for two hours every other week. Occasionally, he helped by doing a second service on Sundays, but he had no other parish responsibility. For this work he got room and board in the rectory. Cooking, cleaning, and laundry were done for him. My monthly rent and food were about $440, and I had to do my own shopping, cooking, laundry, and cleaning. I am prevented from having the job the priest has, though I have equivalent education and extensive experience. I was supported by women's salaries which have averaged about sixty-four cents to every one dollar made by men. Actually, the salaries from our sisters that supported me were less because much service work that they do is underpaid. Systems of sexism are perpetuated by economics. Males are victimized by this as well as females. My brother, who is very fine in elementary education, is now resigning from it because the salary for such work (women's work) will not adequately support his family. Jesus urged the little children to come to him, while others thought time with children would be a bother and a waste. For those who have ears to hear, scripture is a challenge to sexist attitudes and economic systems.

# Notes

## Chapter 1
## Tears, Milk, and Honey

[1]Elisabeth Schussler Fiorenza, *Bread Not Stone, the Challenge of Feminist Biblical Interpretation* (Boston: Beacon Press, 1984), p. 22.

[2]United Nations, *State of the World's Women 1985*, as quoted in *Global Pages*, 3 (August/September 1985):5.

[3]Herb Goldberg, *The Hazards of Being Male: Surviving the Myth of Masculine Privilege* (New York: New American Library, 1976), p. 5.

[4]George Gilder, quoted by James C. Dobson, in *Straight Talk to Men and Their Wives* (Waco, TX: Word, 1980), pp. 156-157.

[5]Liv Ullman, "Forward," in Ruth Leger Sivard, *Women. . .A World Survey* (Washington, D.C.: World Priorities, 1985), p. 3.

[6]Antoinette Clark Wire, "The Miracle Story as the Whole Story," *Southeast Asia Journal of Theology* 22 (1981): 29.

[7]While there is no proof of women's authorship of scripture, these scholars point out the predominance of women's activities, experiences, and viewpoints which suggest women as sources for certain texts and parts of texts: Toni Craven, "Tradition and Convention in the Book of Judith," pp. 49-61, and J. Cheryl Exum, "'You Shall Let Every Daughter Live:' A Study of Exodus 1:8-2:10," pp. 63-82, both in *Semia 28: The Bible and Feminist Hermeneutics*, ed. Mary Ann Tolbert (Chico, CA: Society of Biblical Literature, 1983); Ruth Hoppin, *Priscilla, Author of the Epistle to the Hebrews* (New York: Exposition Press, 1969); Leonard Swidler, *Biblical Affirmations of Woman* (Philadelphia: Westminster Press, 1979), pp. 90-95, on the Song of Songs; Phyllis Trible, *God and the Rhetoric of Sexuality* (Philadelphia: Fortress Press, 1978), pp. 144-166, on the Song of Songs, pp. 166-199, on Ruth. Paul Achtemeier suggests Mark was written by a woman, in *Mark, Proclamation Commentaries* (Philadelphia: Fortress Press, 1975), p. 11.

[8]"Celebration of the Inclusive Language Lectionary," a dialogue sermon of Edwina Hunter and Beclee Newcomer Wilson given on November 16, 1984, at the Pacific School of Religion, as printed in *Journal of Women and Religion* 3 (Summer 1984):7-8.

[9]Victor Turner, *The Ritual Process, Structure and Anti-Structure* (Ithaca, NY: Cornell Paperbacks, 1969), p. vii.

[10]Marcia Eliade, *Rites and Symbols of Initiation* (New York: Harper & Row, 1965), p. 47.

[11]Michael E. Moynahan, S.J., *Once Upon a Parable* (New York: Paulist Press, 1984), p. 5.

[12]Doug Adams, *Humor in the American Pulpit from George Whitefield Through Henry Ward Beecher* (North Aurora, IL: Sharing Co, 1975). pp. 8-9.

[13]Matt Weinstein and Joel Goodman, *Playfair, Everybody's Guide to Noncompetitive Play* (San Luis Obispo, CA: Impact Publishers, 1980), p. 22

[14]*Ibid.*, p. 210.

[15]*Ibid.*, p. 218.

[16]Doug Adams, *Congregational Dancing in Christian Worship* (Austin, TX: Sharing Co., 1971), p. 35.

## Chapter 2
## God Who Mothers

[1]While Hebrew words transliterated into English are often spelled in a variety of ways, within this service the forms of *rechem* and *rachamim* given in Swidler, *Affirmations*, p. 31, have been used.

[2]The poetic prayers of this service usually do not quote scripture directly, but allude to the imagery there. The following references will give the sources of imagery (Deut. 32:18).

[3]Ps. 139:13.

[4]Jer. 31:20.

[5]Isa. 49:15-16.

[6]Isa. 66:13.

[7]Hos. 11:3-4.

[8]Isa. 40:1.

[9]Adapted from Luke 1:26-32, NAB.

[10]John 1:12-13 and 3:4-5.

## Chapter 3, Sarah

[1] Abraham's sacrifice can be compared and contrasted with the sacrifice of Jephthah, a warrior. He told God that he would make a sacrifice if he won a battle. Jephthhah killed his daughter as a sacrifice. The sacrifice of the daughter has been used as a parallel to the sacrifice of Isaac in artistic images prefiguring the eucharistic sacrifice of Christ. See Phyllis Trible in *Texts of Terror* (Philadelphia: Fortress Press, 1984), p. 114. But while Isaac the son was rescued from being killed, the unnamed daughter was not. Thus, could the daughter be considered a stronger symbol of Christ than the son? Why has Christianity been resistant to female symbols of Christ? The same question is raised by a contemporary female symbol of the Christ, a sculpture of a woman on a cross called *Christa*, by Edwina Sandys. For a discussion of thoughts, feelings, and controversies provoked by this female symbol see Edwina Hunter, ed., "Reflections on the *Christa*," *Journal of Woman and Religion*, 4 (Winter 1985).

[2] When Abraham is one hundred and Sarah is ninety, he laughs and questions God's idea of their having a child. God simply continues explaining how this shall happen (Gen. 17:17-18). At Mamre, when Sarah laughs at the idea, it is considered a sign of disrespect and a lack of faith on her part (Gen. 18:13-14).

[3] J. Cheryl Exum writes that Sarah is taken like an object. "'Mother in Israel:' A Familiar Figure Reconsidered," in *Feminist Interpretation of the Bible*, ed. Letty M. Russell (Philadelphia: Westminster Press, 1985), p. 75.

[4] Though more research and reconstruction needs to be done to recover women's stories, in contrast to men's stories about women, in biblical patriarchal texts, initial work has been done by Savina J. Teubal in *Sarah the Priestess, the First Matriarch of Genesis* (Athens, OH: Swallow Press, Ohio University Press, 1984). Teubal theorizes that though many scholars suggest that Sarah lived in the sixteenth-century B.C.E., many of the fragments of the narratives of Sarah, Rebecca, Rachel, and Leah are from much older stories of ancient priestesses and goddesses (pp. 73- 75).

[5] Trible, in her development of the association of the word for God's compassion, *rachamim,* with the word for womb, *rehem,* discusses God's activity through the wombs of Sarah, Leah, Rachel, and Hannah, in *Rhetoric,* pp. 34-35.

[6] Though the biblical text has centered on Abraham, when Sarah finally speaks after four chapters of their saga, as J. Cheryl Exum notes, Sarah controls the action and Abraham obeys her ("'Mother in Israel,'" p. 76).

[7] Though Teubal in *Sarah the Priestess* is not attempting to directly link a historical person, Sarah, with the Code of Hammurabi of 1800 B.C.E., Teubal makes a case for associating Sarah, Rachel, and Leah with priestesses as described in that code (p. 36).

## Chapter 4, Hagar

[1] The biblical text does not indicate Hagar's color, but she is of a different nationality than Abraham and Sarah and a slave. Since one of the most familiar experiences of slavery for a contemporary audience would be that of blacks in America, I have usually done the story identifying Hagar as black. See Phyllis Trible, *Texts of Terror,* p. 35.

[2] The use of the description of the female lover from the Song of Songs, "black and beautiful," is an ironic device. In that biblical story the woman is highly valued by the man and there seems to be a mutual love relationship. That story contrasts with this story of Hagar.

[3] See Gen. 18:22-33 on Abraham, the bargainer.

[4] Hagar being sold for thirty pieces of silver is used as a literary device to associate her with Christ.

[5] In a petition to all governments to implement the United Nations draft resolution 103 concerning recognizing women's work as part of the gross national product, the International Wages for Housework Campaign (King's Cross Women's Centre, 71 Tonbridge St., London WC1, England), states that women do two-thirds of the world's work, while they receive only 5 percent of the world's income. They own less than 1 percent of the world's assets. Women produce, often with the help of children, at least half of the world's food, and this labor is ususally not recognized or paid.

[6] Gen. 12:1. Throughout most of history, wives, dependents, and slaves have been expected to go wherever the father of the family wished to go or found work.

[7] As wives are looked upon as property to bear offspring for their husbands, slaves are looked upon as property to bear offspring for their owners.

[8] In *Diving Deep and Surfacing, Women Writers on Spiritual Quest* (Boston: Beacon Press, 1980), Carol P. Christ describes the dilemma of women in a world in which literature, philosophy, history, and religion have been primarily written by men (p. 5). Women deny their own feelings. Worship sometimes reinforces this suppression and denial.

[9] "Did he take me only to have a male descendant?.... Did he care about me or love me?" are questions that a woman who has some sense of self-worth could ask. A

slave woman in a patriarchal culture probably would not have had enough consciousness of personal worth to even ask such questions.

[10]In an essay, "The Emergence of Black Feminist Consciousness" in *Feminist Interpretation of the Bible,* Katie Geneva Cannon describes the state laws before the Civil War based on *partus sequitur ventrem,* that is, the child follows the mother's status. A child born to a black mother would be a slave. White men often raped black women and laws sanctioned that men did not have to take any responsibility for the offspring (p. 32).

[11]Though the stories of Abraham predate the legal prescriptions of Exodus, the double standards for treatment of male and female slaves is codified there (Exod. 21:2-11). See Leonard Swidler, *Affirmations,* pp. 139-149.

[12]Would a woman of this period have known of abortion? There is no information on this, but information on women having ambivalent feelings about giving birth and the practice of female infanticide are very ancient. Women of classical Greece, as women in some parts of China today (where one's number of children is limited by the government), often let girl infants die, since their societies define females as economic burdens, rather than allowing females to be economic producers. In parts of Africa today, mothers mourn giving birth to girls.

[13]Hagar wonders if she should return to a situation of abuse. This is what contemporary psychologists have called the "battered-wife syndrome." An abused person knows no other reality and considers the abusive situation her own fault.

[14]Trible in a careful analysis of the Hebrew text notes that this sad story of Hagar is made even sadder by the conclusion: A male God listens to the voice of the male child. Hagar, who is the first women in scripture to receive an annunciation and a promise that she will be the ancestor of a great nation, as other women in scripture, loses prominence as her son is emphasized. Her descendants, the Arabs, are looked down upon by Abraham and Sarah's descendants, the Jews (*Texts of Terror,* pp. 25-27).

[15]Hagar cries out for a black God and a mother God. Hagar searches for self-affirmation and meaning. The psychological importance of feminine images of God is noted by the psychologist Toni Wolff in Virginia Ramsey Mollenkott, *The Divine Feminine, the Biblical Imagery of God as Female* (New York: Crossroads, 1984), p. 102.

[16]Hagar searches for a sister God to teach her and Sarah to live as sisters and not as rivals. Patriarchal culture usually defines women in their relationships to fathers, husbands, sons, and sometimes brothers. Women are rewarded for fidelity to men. Conditioning to be faithful to a male deity supports this social practice. The Ruth and Naomi story is an exception to patriarchal literary patterns and it may be an example of a biblical tradition carried on by women.

[17]As at the beginning of this story, the reference to thirty pieces of silver was used as a literary device to associate Hagar with the Christ. At the end "despised and rejected, the outcast of men," a reference to one of the Suffering Servant songs of Isaiah, is used to associate her with the Christ (Isa. 53). See Trible, (*Texts of Terror,* p. 28).

[18]For most of the sources of these statistics, see Ruth Leger Sivard, *Women...A World Survey,* (Washington, D.C.: World Priorities, 1985).

# Chapter 5, Miriam

[1]This imaginative story of Miriam develops the anonymous sister who watched over the baby Moses and the prophetess Miriam as the same person. Aaron, Moses, and Miriam are spoken of as the children of Amram and Jochebed, both of the tribe of Levi (Exod. 6:20). The Song of Miriam (Exod. 15:21) from the J source, is one of the oldest pieces of scripture. See Swidler, *Affirmations,* pp. 86-87. See also, Elisabeth Schussler Fiorenza on the worship of Isis making the power of women equal to that of men in *In Memory of Her, A Feminist Theological Reconstruction of Christian Origins* (New York: Crossroads, 1983), p. 228, and note 71, p. 239.

[2]J. Cheryl Exum writes of the liberation of the Exodus beginning with the stories of women who thwart the pharaoh's attempts to destroy the Hebrew people. ("'You Shall Let Every Daughter Live:' A Study of Exodus 1:8-2:10," *Semia 28, The Bible and Feminist Hermeneutics,* ed. Mary Ann Tolbert [Chico, CA: Society of Biblical Literature, 1983], p. 63).

[3]See Phyllis Trible *Journal of the American Academy of Religion* 41 (1973), as cited in Exum, "Every Daughter," p. 63.

[4]Phyllis Trible extensively discusses the imagery of God as one who gives birth. (*Rhetoric,* p. 64, and cf. pp. 60-71.)

[5]Exum does not specifically say that the first two chapters of Exodus come from women storytellers, but she suggests the possibility ("'You Shall Let Every Daughter Live,'" p. 68). In the Roman Catholic lectionary the story begins with the pharaoh's activity, the verses of the midwives' acts and words are edited out and then the story continues. The lectionary also stops before the mention of Miriam the prophetess leading

the people in praising God. Even what fragments of women's stories survived in patriarchal scripture are cut out in the (even more?) patriarchal editing of the lectionary.

[6]Exum notes the irony of a mother being paid to nurse her own baby ("'A Mother in Israel,'" p. 81).

[7]In Micah 6:4, God says that he sent Moses, Aaron, and Miriam to lead the people.

[8]Miriam, like David (II Sam. 6:14) in a later period, is a leader of song and dance. This may have been a round dance with a repeated chorus as is found in Arab dance today.

[9]Neh. 9:20-21.

[10]Swidler notes that Moses complains to God that he should not have to take care of this difficult people in the wilderness. God gave them birth so God should be the mother taking care of them. (*Affirmations*, p. 30).

[11]Swidler suggests that the story of Miriam being punished while Aaron is not, is designed to discredit her. (*Affirmations*, p. 86).

[12]See note 1, above, about associations between Miriam and the powerful women of Egypt.

[13]Exum reflects on women's leadership in scripture, that though they are rarely major characters, they play crucial roles ("'Mother in Israel,'" p. 85).

[14]Fiorenza, *In Memory of Her*, pp. xiii and 153. The whole book is a feminist theological reconstruction of Christian origins to reclaim women for history and history for women. Fiorenza notes that while we have the name of the man who betrayed Jesus, we have lost the name of this woman who recognized and affirmed Jesus' prophetic identity.

[15]Adams, *Congregational Dancing*, p. 6.

[16]Martha Ann Kirk, C.C.V.I., "Dancing Away Power Structures," *National Catholic Reporter*, 28 October 1983, p. 10. A further development of these ideas on dance as healing and as power can be found in Kirk, *Dancing with Creation: Mexican and Native American Dance in Christian Worship and Education* (Saratoga, CA: Resource Publications, 1983), pp. 16-21 and 94-96.

[17]Adams, *CongregationalDancing*, pp. 86-89 and 60.

# Chapter 6
# Ruth and Naomi

[1]Some scholars say that the book of Ruth was written during the period of Ezra and Nehemiah (450-400 B.C.E.) while there was strong opposition to marrying foreign women. The story is set during the period of the Judges, about 1200-1025 B.C.E. Though the composition of the story is associated with the postexilic period, its language is very ancient and seems to come from the tenth to the eighth century B.C.E. (John Craghan, C.S.S.R. *Esther, Judith, Tobit, Jonah, Ruth* [Wilmington, DE: Michael Glazier, 1982], pp. 198-202). Phyllis Trible uses "she or he" to denote the teller of this story (*Rhetoric*).

[2]Naomi means sweetness or pleasantness. She tells the women of Bethlehem that after all her misfortunes, she should not be called sweet but rather bitter.

[3]John H. Otwell suggests that the Hebrew word for widow *'almanah' comes from lm*, "to be silent." (*And Sarah Laughed* [Philadelphia: Westminster, 1977], pp. 126-127). The association of these destitute ones with the word for silence further develops a major idea of this thesis that women's lack of speech has been a serious lack of power.

[4]Trible notes that the phrase "mother's house" is not expected in patriarchal culture, yet is appropriate here (*Rhetoric*, p. 169).

[5]Trible writes that Naomi calls for the *hesed*, kindness of God. The kindness of women images that of God (*Ibid.*, p. 170).

[6]Each of the independent choices is good. Their freedom and initiative takes on more significance if one compares these three women making choices and initiating action to many other biblical women who are spoken of as passive. For instance, Sarah is "taken" by Abraham to different places.

[7]Ruth like Abraham made a radical decision to leave her native land. Yet Ruth's leap of faith seems to surpass that of Abraham because she has chosen to stay with a female in a world in which worth comes from males.

[8]Ruth clings to Naomi (1:14). This idea of "clinging" is expressive of covenant relationships, a man leaves his parents and *clings* to his wife (Gen. 2:24). Moses urges Israel to *cling* to God (Deut. 10:20, 11:22, and 13:4).

[9]Mollenkott writes that Ruth comes to know the God of Israel through Naomi, and Naomi is in a sense a feminine image of God. Naomi refers to God in 1:20-21, as *Shaddai*, a name which means "the God with breasts." (*Divine Feminine*, p. 57). *Shad* is the Hebrew word for breast, and *-ai* is a feminine ending in Ugaritic, such as on the name Sarai.

[10]Among the many reasons for attributing origins of this book to women storytellers is the scene of the town speaking through its women when Naomi and Ruth ar-

rive and at the end when Naomi cares for her grandchild.

[11]Notice is often made of males bold and strong enough to question the deity. Jacob "wrestles" with God. Job argues extensively. The boldness of Naomi's prayer should be noted. She seems to initiate a court case against Shaddai who has been unfaithful and treated her unjustly.

[12]In Jewish tradition, Ruth is read for Pentecost or Weeks, the period of fifty days that includes the end of the wheat harvest and the beginning of the barley harvest.

[13]If the book of Ruth were written during the time of Nehemiah, there was great hostility toward foreign wives. He cursed the Jewish men who took such wives and had some of them beaten and their hair pulled out (Neh. 13:23 and 25).

[14]The imagery is that of the wings of a mother bird offering protection to her young (Deut. 32:11; Ps. 91:4). Ruth will challenge Boaz to spread his wing over her (Ruth 3:9).

[15]Naomi moves from being the victim to the change agent. The women strategize, initiate, and work boldly.

[16]The Roman Catholic lectionary edits out a large section of the book of Ruth which deals with the women's wisdom, strategy, and initiative. With such editing the story seems to deal with women rescued by the male, Boaz, and the male God. Such editing may be questioned as a serious distortion of this women's story.

[17]A *go-el* is a kinsman who is expected to care for another. This role was so important that during the difficult years of the exile Second Isaiah describes God as a *go'el* (Isa. 41:14, 43:14, and 44:6), according to Otwell (*Sarah Laughed*, p. 131).

[18]Ruth, as Judith and Esther, can be blamed for using physical attractiveness to win men's favor. Yet, in a patriarchal world in which women have often had no power other than physical charm, they might be praised for making the best of a bad situation. Studies are beginning to analyze beauty and women's power.

[19]Naomi tells Ruth to uncover the lower part of Boaz's body. How much she is to uncover remains uncertain, but there are sexual overtones.

[20]While this has been a women's story, Ruth 4:1-12 is an episode in the public, legal, male world. While it has been the initiative of women that has moved the whole story forward, Boaz presents this as a story of men, with the central issue of carrying on the name of the deceased male. Naomi has been concerned about the welfare of Ruth, rather than restoring a male name (*Rhetoric*, p. 192).

[21]After the male episode, the story again focuses on women. Trible writes that it is a story of justice for living females more than justice for dead males. (*Ibid.*, p. 194).

# Chapter 7, Susanna

[1]Susanna means 'lily' and probably suggests her freshness and beauty. This word is frequently used in the Song of Songs (2:1, 2, 16; 4:5; 6:2-3; and 7:3).

[2]The Susanna story is the only example in scripture of a rape being discussed as an offense against the woman herself. All of the other examples of sexual abuse and assault are concerned with violating the property rights of the males who "possessed" the women. See Maria Marshall Fortune's *Sexual Violence, the Unmentionable Sin* (New York: Pilgrim Press, 1983), pp. 55-56 and 60. Biblical commentaries usually have discounted Susanna's experience and focused on the hero Daniel or on the community learning moral lessons of virtue (chastity) triumphing over vice. My interest has been in Susana's independent, heroic action, her choice for integrity even if it meant death. She could be compared to Christ, whose choice for integrity brought death. I have not quoted the confusing biblical text which says that she chooses to die "rather than sin," because being the victim of a rape is not sinning.

[3]The story may be a Pharisaic polemic against the Sadducees. If the second century community had this story why was it not accepted as Canon by the Jews at the Council of Jamnia? David M. Kay suggests that the story would not be popular with elders and they are the ones who fixed the Canon: See Cary A. Moore, *Daniel, Esther & Jeremiah: The Additions, the Anchor Bible* (Garden City, N.J.: Doubleday, 1977) pp. 13, 80, 81, 87.

[4]The bath scene is not in the Septuagint version. The version of the Susanna story most widely distributed today and the one used in this project from the New American Bible and the Anchor Bible come from the Greek version of scriptures known as the "Theodotion," and not the Septuagint. Why is the "Theodotion" used more? The "Theodotion" focuses on Daniel more; in the Septuagint, Susanna is more central. One version of the Septuagint has the story of Susanna as the opening of the book of Daniel. Probably it was not considered appropriate to have this story focused on a woman to open the collection of the hero Daniel, therefore, it was both put in the last chapter and it was replaced by the version giving him more importance than her. Moore even suggests that an early version of this story may not have mentioned Daniel at all (Moore, *Daniel*, pp. 80, 90-91, 109, and 115-116).

[5]The Hebrews had stories that during the Babylonian captivity, evil men would seduce women by telling them that they had the seed of the Messiah. If the women would have intercourse with them, they could bear the Messiah who could free the people. The Susanna story may be related to these stories. (Jan Braverman, *Jerome's Commentary on Daniel: A Study of Comparative Jewish and Christian Interpretations of the Hebrew Bible* [Washington, DC: Catholic Biblical Association of America, 1978], pp. 126-127).

[6]Susanna might have thought, "My children need a mother so it is best for me not to be stoned, therefore I will have to suffer this rape." Would she have felt guilty? Institutional structures and social custom have often reinforced this undeserved guilt in women. Women who have been socialized as the caretakers of others and as responsible for others frequently have fluid ego boundaries and attribute to themselves guilt. See Rosemary Radford Ruether, "Misogynism and Virginal Feminism in the Fathers of the Church," in *Religion and Sexism*, ed. by Rosemary Radford [New York: Simon & Schuster, 1974], pp. 151-183). The one-time victim of rape, as well as the battered woman, often suffers from a lack of self-esteem which is grounded in being raised in patriarchal culture in which males are valued more than females. See Susan Brooks Thistlethwaite, "Every Two Minutes: Battered Women and Feminist Interpretation," *Feminist Interpretation of the Bible*, pp. 96-107.

[7]The law stating that stoning is the penalty for adultery is found in Lev. 20:10. Also, Ezek. 16:38-40 and John 8:5 refer to this. The only specific account in the Bible of trial by ordeal is if a husband suspects his wife of adultery. There is no similar trial for a man, and even if she is found innocent, no guilt will be attached to the husband, but the woman shall bear the penalty of her guilt (Num. 5:14-31).

[8]Susanna is described as "beautiful and God-fearing" (Dan. 13:2), and these same words are used of other women from about the same period of literature of the Septuagint: Judith (Judith 8:7-8), Sarah (Tobit 6:12 and 3:14-15), and Esther (Esther 2:7 and 20 of the Septuagint).

[9]The elders want Susanna dead since they cannot rape her. Can they or any man who tries to rape a woman be said to "love the woman?" Is it love or violence which prompts rape? In "More Power Than We Want: Masculine Sexuality and Violence," *Reweaving the Web of Life, Feminism and Non-Violence*, (Philadelphia: New Society Publishers, 1982), Bruce Kokopeli and George Lakey write, that patriarchy has shaped men to express dominance through sexuality (pp. 232-233).

[10]While the translation speaks of the elders wishing to unveil her, the original text probably meant "stripped naked" since, according to Ezek. 16:37-39, such was part of the penalty for adultery (cf. also Hosea 2:3 and 10). That a woman not convicted but *merely suspected* of sexual sin would be treated so cruelly by the persons who were supposed to be the guardians of law and religion seems appalling; yet, sad examples of contemporary guardians' attitudes and actions could be given. Fortune writes of the Spokane police captain who is in charge of the investigations of rape cases. When he was publicly asked what advice he would give to women worried about the increasing number of rapes in the area, he replied, "Lay back and enjoy it." (Fortune, *Sexual Violence*, pp. 30 and 41).

[11]In contrast with the book of Ruth which has extensive direct and indirect discourse by the women characters, only five of the sixty-two verses of the scriptural story of Susanna are her words. I do not think the story as it is written in scripture is a women's story, but rather men's story about a woman. For instance, the story closes, saying that the family praised God and that Daniel was greatly esteemed. The man is esteemed. God is praised for the woman. This is male-centered narrative. "Neutral" narrative might say, "God was praised for the good deeds of Susanna and of Daniel," or "Daniel and Susanna were both esteemed by the people."

[12]Rape in this service is used a metaphor for all relationships of domination. The association is not made casually, but deliberately growing out of a conviction that rape is a central act of violence in the world. Coming to understand rape may be getting at the specific metaphysical problems from which patriarchal culture suffers.

# Chapter 8, Daughter

[1]Swidler notes the emphasis placed on ritual purity. The Mishnah said if a priest served at the altar while he was unclean, the other priests took him outside the Temple and split open his brain with clubs (*Affirmations*, p. 148).

[2]Lev. 15:25-27.

[3]Discussion of the contemporary practice and women's feelings about the *mikvah*, or ritual bath, which marks a woman's transition from the unclean state of menstruation, *tumah*, to the clean state, *tahara*, is given in Roslyn Lacks, *Women and Judaism, Myth, History, and Struggle* (Garden City, NY: Doubleday, 1980), pp. 152-158.

[4]Barbara Zannotti, in "Is Peace Possible in a Patriarchal Society?" explores the theory that women

who have had physical bonds with children in the womb and who are responsible for most of the childcare have a highly developed sense of relationship with their children and people in general. Men do not have as highly developed a sense of relationship with people and tend to relate to people more abstractly. When societies are patriarchal, that is, when those in power are those who live in abstractions more than in direct relationships with others, war can take place. (*Probe 6* [October/November 1982]:1-2).

[5]Jer. 31:15.

[6]Were women tellers or writers of these two stories about women? Paul Achtemeier has written that Mark may have been written by a woman. Elisabeth Schussler Fiorenza refers to the author as "s/he," and she notes the crucial roles women play throughout the gospel (Fiorenza, *In Memory of Her*, pp. 60 and 316-323).

[7]In the Jerusalem Temple, women were only allowed in the Court of the Women, which was between the Court of the Gentiles and the Court of Israel, to which only men were admitted. Women could only enter their outer area through certain gates and they could not come into the Temple area at all for seven days following their menstruation, or within forty days after the birth of a boy, or twice as long—eighty days—after the birth of a girl.

[8]In Mark's gospel the word for suffering used of the woman (Mark 5:26) is the word used of Jesus' passion (Mark 8:31 and 9:12). The suffering of this woman was similar to that which Jesus experienced before his death.

[9]Swidler, in *Affirmations*, writes, though there were stories of rabbis who healed, they did not heal women (p.180).

[10]Mark 1:30-31.

[11]Mark 2:41 tells of a leper being cured through touch. This Greek word for touch is used only three times in Mark's gospel. In using the same word for the leper story and the story of the bleeding woman, the author may be associating the stories. The laws concerning the impurity of women are more restrictive than those concerning men (Swidler, *Affirmations*, pp. 148-149).

[12]Luke 4:18, based on Isa. 61.

[13]Antoinette Clark Wire asks the basic question of why the miracle stories were told (before being incorporated in the larger literary structures of the gospels). If their main point was to praise the healer for the miracle, they would have extensive doxologies, yet they do not. The stories invite the listeners to break out of a closed world. Wire describes the hemorrhaging woman's story among the "demand stories" in which the needy person takes an active role. "Demand stories" are important for contemporary women or other members of oppressed groups. They cannot passively wait for God to liberate them; they are called to become active subjects, to live out "demand stories." ("The Structures of the Gospel Miracle Stories and Their Tellers," *Semia*, nos. 11-12 [1978]:106-108).

[14]Mark 5:1-20.

[15]The Book of Numbers states that people are to place tassels on the corners of their garments to remind them of God's laws (Num. 16: 39-40).The tassel that should remind one of God's laws is what the woman touched. Her touch violated the law. Herman Waetjen discusses this story as found in Matthew's gospel as the seventh of ten great works of Jesus. The healing may be symbolic of Israel's freedom from the law and the bondage and separtion it often imposes. (*The Origin and Destiny of Humanness* [Corte Madera, CA: Omega Books, 1976], p. 126). The raising of the girl is the eighth work of Jesus, an expectation of apocalyptic eschatology, a new beginning.

[16] The uniqueness of the woman's miracle is that, takes place solely at the woman's initiative (5:28-29). Jesus feels his flow of power that stops her flow of blood (5:30).

[17]The legal definition of the woman as ritually impure can be associated with the contemporary Catholic position that woman are somehow unfit to preside at sacramental rituals, to touch the Body of Christ in the Eucharist.

[18]Gerd Theissen points out that the cure of the woman with the issue of blood (Mark 5:24b-34; Matt. 9:20-22; and Luke 8:42b- 48) is the only miracle story other than the stilling of the storm in which all three synoptic gospels talk about faith (*The Miracle Stories of the Early Christian Tradition*, trans. Francis McDonnagh [Edinburgh: T. & T. Clark, 1983], p. 133).

[19] This story is similar to the story of Lazarus. In both, the delay allows time for the person to die and thus heightens the suspense and the greatness of the miracle.

[20]John 11:26.

[21]In a discussion of the *basileia* or reign or state of *shalom* to which God invites us, Fiorenza writes that Jesus in touching the dead body of the little girl would have become unclean (Num. 19:11-13), but both the woman and the girl are given a new life of eschatological well-being. (*In Memory of Her*, p. 124).

# Chapter 9
# Mary of Magdala

[1]Despite the confusion of Magdalene with the woman who was a sinner, in the western church there has also been a tradition of her as the *apostola apostolorum*. Such references can be seen in writings such as Hippolytus of Rome, Rabanus Maurus, and Bernard of Clairvaux. Until the liturgical reforms of Vatican II, the Creed was recited on the feasts of the twelve male apostles and of Mary Magdalene (Swidler, *Affirmations*, p. 209).

[2]In *The Women Around Jesus* (New York: Crossroad, 1982), Elizabeth Moltmann-Wendel writes that the sinner spoken of in Luke 7 and Mary Magdalene, the apostle, have as little to do with each other as Judas and Peter. Moltmann-Wendel also develops the idea that as Christians in the past have projected the sin of Judas onto the whole Jewish people, so sexual sin has been projected onto women (pp.64-65).

[3]In the Catholic Sunday lectionary, the passage of Christ's conversation with Mary Magdalene, probably the most important passage in scripture in affirming women's commission to evangelize, is omitted. The passage speaks of Peter and John, then stops. I have volunteered five times to share her story in parishes for Easter worship. Though priests complain of being overworked from all the services of Holy Week, my offer of help has not been accepted.

[4]Brown describes what designates an apostle, seeing the risen Christ and being sent to proclaim him (see I Cor. 9:1-2 and 15:8-11; and Gal. 1:11-16). Though some communities believed that Peter had apostolic primacy because he was the first to see the risen Christ, the Johannine author writes that Mary Magdalene was the first to see him (Raymond E. Brown, S.S., *The Community of the Beloved Disciple* [New York: Paulist Press, 1979], pp. 189-190).

[5]Moltmann-Wendel writes that the "evil spirits" indicate a mental illness, as manic depression or epilepsy. She continues to explain that the patriarchal church has confused the woman who was a sinner (Luke 8) and the women who anointed Jesus (Mark 14 and John 12) with Mary Magdalene. The image of Mary as a sexual sinner was created by males and kindles male fantasies (*The Women Around Jesus*, pp. 66-67). Moltmann-Wendel then gives examples of art and literature through the ages which have defamed Mary, but also examples which have depicted her as an apostle preaching in churches and other places.

[6]Defining "demons" or defining weakness or sin for women has been one of the main tasks of feminist spirituality. While traditional patriarchal spirituality has usually defined pride as the greatest sin, women's predominant fault has usually been a lack of self-esteem.

[7]See Bernadette J. Brooten, *Women Leaders in the Ancient Synagogue* (Chico, CA: Scholars Press, 1982), pp. 141-144. Though Brooten is not specifically discussing the women around Jesus who supported him and his friends out of their means, her discussion of inscriptions about women who were donors to and of synagogues gives some context for the women who financed Jesus (p. 143).

[8]Mary and other women were healed and then they followed Jesus (Luke 8). None of the men healed by Jesus leave all to follow him. Moltmann-Wendel writes that society must have found these women challenging (*The Women Around Jesus*, p. 69).

[9]Early texts give hints of women's roles in the Jesus movement and early Christian communities. Fiorenza traces the efforts of patriarchy to repress women as prophets and teachers. Among the texts mentioning the women as those sent to proclaim are the *Epistola Apostolorum*, the *Sophia Jesu Christi*, the *Gospel of Philip*, the *Gospel of the Egyptians*, the *Great Questions of Mary*, the *Gospel of Mary*, and the *Pistis Sophia*. In the last work, Mary Magdalene asks thirty-nine of the forty-six questions and is a major interpreter of revelation. Peter is hostile toward her and debates her authority. This debate can also be seen in the second-century *Gospel of Mary*. She is recounting the revelations that she has received and Peter objects. These writings reflect the debate in the early church whether women should teach (*In Memory of Her*, pp. 304-306).

[10]Fra Angelico, the Italian Renaissance painter, in *The Prayer of Jesus in the Garden of Gethsemane*, a fresco in the Monastery of San Marco in Florence, depicts Jesus praying in the upper left, Peter, James, and John sleeping nearby, and Martha and Mary praying in the right foreground. See Moltmann-Wendel, *The Women Around Jesus*, pp. 30 and 37-38.

[11]This story may echo the Song of Songs 3:1-4 in which the woman rises early seeking her beloved. She asks the watchman. When she finds her friend, she holds him and will not let him go.

[12]The Greek verb "to seek" in the question, "Woman, whom do you seek?" can mean "to study" and "to engage in the activities of a disciple," according to Fiorenza. Magdalene responds as a disciple and recognizes Christ as "Rabboni," as the "teacher." Fiorenza notes that Mary Magdalene as Mary of Nazareth, the nameless Samaritan woman, Martha, and Mary of Bethany belongs to Jesus' very own disciples. The evangelist, who may have been a woman, gives

these five women as examples of discipleship *(In Memory of Her*, p. 333).

[13]As the disciples on the road to Emmaus do not recognize Christ until he breaks bread, so Mary Magdalene does not recognize him until he calls her by name. Brown suggests that Luke is indicating the Eucharist is a way of knowing the presence of Christ, and John is indicating the spoken word is a way of knowing the presence of Christ *(The Anchor Bible*, p. 1009).

[14]Moltmann-Wendel writes that previously there has been little reflection on women's experiences of God. Male disciples betray Jesus and male theology often involves the dialectic between betrayal and conversion. Mary Magdalene's experience does not involve conversion or betrayal, but rather healing; Magdalene seeks intimacy. Women's conflict may be in holding on or letting go. *(The Women Around Jesus, p. 72).*

## Chapter 10, Martha

[1]This story of a visit to Martha and Mary does not appear in any of the other gospels and seems to come from Luke's special source "L." The Lukan community may have had contact with the Johannine community and known of the stories of Jesus' visits with Martha and Mary, but there is no way of being certain. Both Luke's and John's communities remembered two women who were close to Jesus and different in their gifts.

[2]Eugene LaVerdiere writes that the journey to Jerusalem is a symbolic journey to God's fullness. Martha is the hostess for a meal with Jesus along the journey. *(The New Testament in the Life of the Church* [Notre Dame: Ave Maria Press, 1980], pp. 102-103). Jesus does not tell Martha to stop her service, but to avoid being anxious and upset. Martha is a leader of the Christian community of the 80s who hosts table fellowship (what comes to be called Eucharist) in her home. This is a reminder for women and men who do this to keep their focus on Christ in these celebrations and not be lost in the details of hospitality.

[3]For a discussion of Rabbi Eliezer's comment, see Fiorenza, *In Memory of Her*, pp. 108, 217, and 238. I, like Fiorenza, do not wish to make a contrast suggesting that Judaism was patriarchal and Christianity was not. Society has been patriarchal; within it there have been both individual Jews and individual Christians who have expressed patriarchy and others who have broken with it.

[4]The expression used of Mary, that she "sat at the Lord's feet" is a technical phrase meaning that one studies with a rabbi. Women were usually not allowed

to study like this, so Jesus' approval of her is amazing. He is saying that women have a right to study theology like men; they do not have to be confined to domestic tasks.

[5]This is given in the daily prayers for Jewish males as cited in Swidler, *Affirmations*, p. 155.

[6]In a discussion of Martha's conversation with Jesus about her brother Lazarus' death, Moltmann-Wendel writes that Martha is strong and assertive. Many would consider her "unfeminine." This story develops her personality as suggested by Moltmann-Wendel. *(The Women Around Jesus*, p. 24).

[7]Martha makes a faith profession similar to Peter's (Matt. 16:15-19). Fiorenza writes that Martha represents the apostolic faith of the Johannine community, just as Peter did for the Matthean community. The raising of Lazarus is the climax of Jesus' "signs," and comes right before Jesus dies. Fiorenza writes that possibly the evangelist put these words into the mouth of Martha as the faith confession of a disciple to identify her with the writer of the gospel *(In Memory of Her*, p. 330).

[8]Both this story at Martha and Mary's home and the story recorded in John 12:1-9 have eucharistic overtones which indicate the communities' association of that sacramental meal with women hosts, women ministers. In regard to the meal mentioned in John, Sandra Schneiders notes that it took place on a Sunday evening, the usual time for Eucharist in the early church (Sandra M. Schneiders, I.H.M., "Women in the Fourth Gospel and the Role of Women in the Contemporary Church," *BiblicalTheology Bulletin*, 12 [April 1982]:41-42). The Johannine community may have had foot-washing in its eucharistic liturgy.

[9]Brown writes that saying there were no women "priests" in New Testament times is not accurate. In Christian scriptures the term is applied to Christians *only* in the broad sense of the priesthood of the people (I Peter 2:5; Rev 5:10). Brown continues to discuss the more specific issue of whether women celebrated the Eucharist. There is very little known about who presided. There is some evidence that prophets did (Acts 13:2; *Didache* 10:7). Women did prophesy (I Cor. 11:5; Acts 21:9), so perhaps they presided *(Community of the Beloved Disciple*, pp. 184-185). The *Didache* states that prophets should be permitted to offer "prayers of thanksgiving" as they wish. "Prayers of thanksgiving" is the term used for Eucharist, which means 'thanksgiving'. David E. Aune cites this as an example of the extraordinary freedom which was allowed to prophets *(Prophecy in Early Christianity and the Ancient Mediterranean World*, [Grand Rapids, MI:

William B. Eerdmans Publishing Co., 1983], pp. 196 and 402).

[10]The four unmarried daughters of Philip who prophesied are mentioned in Acts 21:8-9. For a discussion of prophets as a recognizable group within the community who shared their revelations within worship in Corinth in the first century, see Aune, *Prophecy in Early Christianity*, pp. 198-199. Women were among those who prophesied in Corinth. Fiorenza focuses on women and prophesy (*In Memory of Her*, pp. 226-233).

[11]For a discussion of the importance of house churches in early Christianity and women's roles in them, see Fiorenza, *In Memory of Her*, pp. 175-184.

[12]Dennis Ronald MacDonald (*The Legend and the Apostle, the Battle for Paul in Story and Canon* [Philadelphia: Westminster Press, 1983]) develops the theory that the *Acts of Paul* and other legends originated in stories told by women in which Christianity gives women great freedom to be teachers, itinerant evangelists, and celibate. The stories say that Paul invites and commissions the women. The women often leave traditional patriarchal households in which they are under men and care for men's offspring. MacDonald suggests that parts of the pastoral epistles were written in reaction to these women's stories. The epistles wanted to put women "back in their place," for example, I Tim. 2:11, 12, 15 and Titus 2:3b-5 (*Legend*, pp. 58, 59, 77). Fiorenza also develops the household codes as a suppression of women's freedom in Christianity (*In Memory of Her*, pp. 251-284).

[13]Brooten studied tomb inscriptions of the Roman and Byzantine periods which referred to Jewish women as: (1) heads of synagogues; (2) as leaders; (3) as elders; (4) as "mothers of the synagogue"; and (5) as priests. She also studied other ancient sources pertaining to these titles. When the titles were given to men, traditional patriarchal scholarship has said that the titles were functional. When the titles were given to women, traditional scholarship has said that the titles were only honorific and that women did not function in those ways. Yet, Brooten's conclusion is that the fact that traditional scholarship has denied the leadership of these women does not mean the women were not leaders; instead, the scholarship reveals the biased perspective of a patriarchal approach. (Brooten, *Women Leaders*, p. 150).

[14]MacDonald, in developing a thesis that the *Acts of Paul* originated from women storytellers in Asia Minor, writes that women exercised more leadership on that subcontinent than anywhere else in the early church. He cites the deacon Phoebe, the female apostle (Junia; Rom. 16:7), several church workers (Priscilla, Mary, Tryphaena, Tryphosa, and Persis; vv. 3, 6, and 12), and others (the mother of Rufus, the sister of Nereus, and Julia; vv. 13 and 15). He also mentions Priscilla, Apphia, and Nympha from scripture, and other women mentioned in other sources (*Legend*, pp. 37-38). For a discussion of women's activities that can be gleaned from scripture, see Fiorenza, *In Memory of Her*, pp. 166-175.

[15]See I Cor. 11:17-34.

[16]Fiorenza notes that the Christian gospel cannot be proclaimed if the women disciples and their activities are omitted. Thus, feminists are in the process of reclaiming the supper at Bethany. An all-male Last Supper is a betrayal of true Christian discipleship. *In Memory of Her*, p. xiv).

[17]Marianne Sawicki writes that the Talmud gives three personal services that a wife rather than servants did for her husband. She washed his face, hands, and feet. Peter was upset that Jesus was acting like a wife (John 13:3-6). Peter understands this, for he offers his head and hands with his feet (*Faith and Sexism* [New York: Seabury Press, 1979], p. 32).

[18]"The Round Dance of the Cross," a ritual for sacred dance, is in the *Acts of John*, an early document. See Elaine H. Pagels, "To the Universe Belong the Dancer," *Parabola, Myth and Quest for Meaning*, 4 (May 1979):6-9. For a discussion of the development of hierarchy and the suppression of dance, see Doug Adams, *Congregational Dancing*, p. 35.

# Chapter 11, Dorcas

[1]Ernest Haechen, in *The Acts of the Apostles, a Commentary* (Philadelphia: Westminster Press, 1971), writes that in the synoptic healing stories the names of those healed is not given. Can the use of "Tabitha called Dorcas" indicate that the author wished to convey not only that God healed through Jesus power, but also that she was a significant person for the community? The Greek word calling her a disciple (9:36) is the only example of the feminine form of this word in Christian scriptures. This expression is elaborated by praising her charity and good works. She was a person who gave alms and is not to be confused with the recipients of alms (p. 339). While not dealing directly with the story of Dorcas, Bernadette Brooten extensively discusses women who financially support religion and give leadership, see *Women Leaders*. Luke's mention of Mary of Magdala and the other women who supported Jesus and his companions (Luke 8:1-3) and of Lydia the businesswoman who hosted Paul (Acts 16:13-15 and 40) gives a little information on women and economics. See also Evelyn and Frank Stagg (*Women in the World of Jesus* [Philadelphia: Westminster Press, 1978], p. 228). The women do not

directly ask for her restoration, but show samples of how much good she has done to move Peter. This story is told like the miracle stories of I Kings 17:17ff and II Kings 4:32ff, but Peter does not touch a woman as Elijah and Elisha touch boys. His words are identical with those of Jesus in Mark 5, so, though Peter does not mention the name of Jesus, this is evidently calling forth his healing power. As in II Kings 4:35 and Luke 7:15, "She opened her eyes" (Haechen, *Acts of the Apostles*, pp. 339-340). Haechen speaks of the widows as the poor who benefited from Dorcas' work and that is why they pleaded for her. Could she have been the leader of a group of widows who did kind deeds for others?

[2] Since the Chilean military coup d'etat in 1973, resistance has been in many forms. During the coup, over 30,000 were killed, 100,000 imprisoned, 2,500 disappeared and over 1,000,000—10 percent of the population—fled. Women, particularly those who have lost family members, have worked in church- based tapestry workshops and told their stories in the designs of the tapestries called *arpilleras* revealing hunger, minimal housing, unemployment, disappeared family members, and exiles. The tapestries are smuggled out of the country.

[3] For extensive examples of the variety, importance, and beauty of women's fiber arts through the ages, see Judy Chicago with Susan Hill, *Embroidering Our Heritage, the Dinner Party Needlework* (Garden City, NY: Anchor Books, 1980).

[4] Of all the exhibits that the Oakland Museum has ever organized, the most well-attended one was "Quilts and Women's Lives." The exhibit was organized around times of transition or "rites of passage." It had quilts made in each period and gave excerpts from women's dairies and statements about the significance of the process of creation, of the creations, and of the relationships involved. The exhibit is described in *American Quilts: A Handmade Legacy*, edited by L. Thomas Frye (Oakland, CA: The Oakland Museum, 1981).

[5] Valerie Quinney, "Textile Women: Three Generations in the Mill," *Southern Exposure* 34 (Winter 1976):66-72.

[6] Maria Riley, "Women Workers in the Global Factory," *Center Focus* no. 52 (January 1983):3.

[7] God made clothes of skins for the people (Gen. 3:21).

[8] In Hebrew society, providing food, water, and clothing was women's work. In the desert, God takes care of these women's tasks (Neh. 9:20-21).

[9] God clothes the lilies (Luke 12:27-28).

[10] Lark Books Staff and Marianne Philban, eds. *The Ribbon, a Celebration of Life* (Asheville, NC: Lark Books, 1985). In 1982, Justine Merritt suggested people making squares of about three by two feet of things that they valued and would want to preserve, in other words, their motivation for seeking peace in the world. Patriarchal legend describes St. George, the male hero, confronting a dragon and slaying it. In contrast, St. Martha met the dragon, tamed it, tied her girdle around its neck, and led it home. Hurty suggested that the Peace Ribbon is Martha's girdle which we tie around the Pentagon (Kathleen Hurty, "Power in a New Key: Excerpts from Purdue," *Concern*, 28 [January 1986]:36-37. Also see Elisabeth Moltmann-Wendel, *The Women Around Jesus* (New York: Crossroad, 1982), pp. 13-48. Parts of the Peace Ribbon can now be seen in the Peace Museum, 367 W. Erie Street, Chicago, IL.

[11] Margaret Mead, *Male and Female: A Study of the Sexes in a Changing World* (New York: Morrow Paperback, William Morrow & Co., 1949, 1975), pp. 159-160.

# Appendix: Music for the Services

## 1. RACHAMIM, COMPASSION

In the Jewish tradition, people praying often sway back and forth as a way of more deeply involving their whole selves in prayer. This prayer "dance" is called "shuckling," and may be done slowly or quickly.

The movement to this dance is very simple, inviting one to quiet meditation and the kind of intimate relationship with God that an unborn child has with the mother. Fold your arms over your chest, close your eyes, and gently sway back and forth.

Refrain:
Ra-cha-mim Com-pas-sion, Ra-cha-mim, Ra-cha-mim Womb of God, Com-pas-sion Ra-cha-mim, Ra-cha-mim!

1. As a mother com-forts her child, so will I com-fort you, pre-cious one. (to refrain)

2. E-ven if a mo-ther for-gets her own child yet ev-ery mo-ment you'll be __ cared for by me. (to refrain)

3. Com-fort my peo-ple, for I hear their cries, and I will hold them close, __ tears in my eyes. (to refrain)

by Colleen Fulmer
© 1985

84

## 2. BLESSED IS SHE

by Colleen Fulmer
© 1985

Luke 1:39-55 says that even the unborn child John leapt in his mother's womb. Mary and Elizabeth must have leapt and danced for joy also, for a new creation was promised in which the social order was transformed, the lowest being empowered.

Chorus: Begin with your hands and arms crossed at the wrist against your breast, a traditional posture of prayer often shown in paintings of Mary. On "who believed that....," open your hands and arms straight out in front, palms up as if open to and receiving from God, and then bring your hands all the way down. On the first "would be fulfilled," sweep your right hand up over your head, and on the second, sweep your left hand up.

Verses: Joyfully skip and dance all around the room freely led by the Spirit. If you like more structure, get in pairs, link elbows and skip in a circle. On the next verse, get a new partner.

### 3. SARAH'S SONG

**4. RUAH**

by Colleen Fulmer
© 1985

Refrain:

Ru- ah,____ Ru- ah,___ breath of God with- in us___ Ru- ah,____

Ru- ah,___ Spir- it of our God.

1. The Spir-it of God with-in us crum-bles the an-cient walls, build-ing a new cre-a-tion, the ci-ty of our God. (to refrain)

2. Have no fear with-in you, for I will be your strength.____ The bar-ren will be fruit-ful,___ the la-me shall dance and leap.____ (to refrain)

3. Your po-wer will come to full-ness in the weak and hum-ble child, from the roots of the small-est flo-wer___ to the hearts of the old and wise.____ (to refrain)

4)    Am     G     Dm     Am

4. Old men will see their vis-ions,   young men will dream their dreams.___

Dm     Am     G     Am

Wom-en will be our pro-phets,___ with child-ren in the lead.___ (to refrain)

5)    Am     G     Dm     Am

5. A wis-dom en-fleshed in Je-sus___ grace that moves a- new___ en-

Dm     Am     G     Am

Kin-dled in a peo-ple, the ma-ny and the few___ (to refrain)

6)    Am     G     Dm     Am

6. The Dance of all cre-a-tion,___ Sing-er of liv-ing song,___

Dm     Am     G     Am

Beau-ty from days e-ter-nal,___ the praise of a lov-ing God.___ (to refrain)

7)    Am     G     Dm     Am

Root of the stem of Jes-se,___ tree with arms so strong,___

Dm     Am     G     Am

life that grows through dy-ing,___ re-veal-ing a ten-der God.___ (to refrain)

*Ruah,* the feminine Hebrew word, means breath, wind, or spirit. The first image of God in scripture is that of the moving, dancing creative Spirit hovering over the chaos bringing forth life. The image suggests a mother bird hovering over her brood.

Though this dance may be done in places with fixed chairs or pews, simply moving toward one side and then the other, it is most fun when done in a circle.

Chorus: Hold your arms up in front of your body, a little above shoulder height. Imagine where your hands are as the center of a figure eight on its die. Trace the left loop of a figure 8 on the first "Ruah" and the right loop on the second "Ruah," then raise your arms above your head and let them burst open and come down palms facing up. Repeat on the second line.

Verses: Hold hands, walk to the right on the first two lines. (A more confident group may walk doing the grapevine step, that is, right foot step to the side, left step across in front, right foot step to the side, left step across in back, etc.)

On the third line, walk in toward the center, raising arms. On the last line, walk back out, lowering arms.

## 5. REST IN MY WINGS

by Colleen Fulmer
© 1985

Invite people to meditate on times of darkness or challenges in their lives when they lack direction. After a little while, explain that the lights will be turned out (have a few candles burning). All are invited to freely dance in the darkness, letting the Spirit lead and shelter them. After this, invite people to share feelings of dancing in the darkness without direction.

## 6. WE ARE THE BODY OF CHRIST

text by Martha Ann KIRK, CCVI
music by Colleen Fulmer ©1985

Refrain:

We are the body of Christ, Birth-ing, Feed-ing, Touch-ing Weep-ing. We are the Body of Christ, Mend-ing, Bleed-ing, Heal-ing, Danc-ing. Glo-ri-fy God in our bo-dies, Dance with God through our lives

1. Birth from our bo-dies as birth of Christ's Spi-rit, bring-ing life to the world.

2. Our breast milk in nurs-ing, as blood from Christ's side, quench-ing thirst by grace.

3. The touch of our kind-ness as that from Christ's hands, mak-ing peace for our world.

4. The tears from our eyes, as those shed by Christ, wash-ing dark-ness a-way.

5. Mend-ing the tear, as for-give-ness Christ shares, bring-ing peace to our world.——(ref.)

6. Blood from our hearts, as wine shared by Christ, chang-ing death to new life.——(to refrain)

7. Bread from our hands, as loaves shared by Christ, feed-ing all those in need.——

8. Dance of our lives, as joy sung by Christ, free-ing all for new life.——

Women in their daily activities (or daily dances) image Christ's sacramental activities (birthing and washing in baptism; healing, uniting, mending and touching in Reconciliation and Anointing; feeding in Eucharist; all are metaphors of activity that have been done especially by women.   Although the *Vatican Declaration on the Ordination of Women* states that women do not physically resemble Christ, and this is why they may not be ordained, to image the fullness of the Body of the Risen Christ, women are needed.

Chorus: During the first line, begin with arms by your side and slowly bring your hands up your body until they rest over your heart.  On the second line, as if you are holding gifts of service from your heart in your hands, slowly reach your hands forward and out, giving and sharing.

On the third line, raise your arms high, then come down, hands touching your face and body until your hands rest on your heart.  On the fourth line, repeat the movements of the second line.  On the fifth line, repeat the movements of the second line.  On the last line, with arms still above your head, sway right, left, right, left.

Verses: You may stand in place and sway or walk in a circle holding hands.

# 7. CHOOSE LIFE

a capella

by Colleen Fulmer
©1985

Refrain:

Choose life that we might live — Choose peace, that we might see — a to-mor-row.

Let Justice roll — Roll like a ri-ver, Flow like a river down. _____

1) 1. It's a pow-er-ful love — that's mov-in' a moun-tain, a pow-er-ful love —

— that casts out fear, a pow-er-ful love — dis-arm-in' the na-
(to refrain)

— tions, the pow-er is now _____ that love is here _____

2) 2. It's a liv-in hope — seek-in' for — to-mor-row, a liv-in hope

— Know-in' pro-mise in pain, — A liv-in' hope — that's fight-in' op-pres-
(to refrain)

— sion, Giv-in' the poor _____ their rights a-gain _____

3)

3. It's a grow-in' faith __ giv-in' birth to free— dom, Grow-in' in faith

__ stand-in hand in hand __ a grow-in in faith __ mov-in' us to ac-
(to refrain)

__ -tion sing-in' o' plen - ty, the fruit of the land. ____

4)

4. It's a mov-in' spir- it meets the strug-gle Lead-in' the dance

__ that's stir-rin' the flame and mov-in' the hearts in-side o' the peo-
(to refrain)

__ -ple bring-in' the dead ___ to life __ a-gain ____

## 8. MIRIAM'S SONG

by Colleen Fulmer
© 1986

2)

2. We'll shout "No" to their systems, their wars and bombs and guns, We'll clasp our hands as daugh-ter, as mother,___ sisters, sons, we'll stand as one___ We'll stand as one___ to guard our children from their mad-ness, we'll stand as one. lai lai lai lai lai lai lai lai lai___ (So)

3)

3. We're exiles___ from our nations for they have cho-sen death, But we will work for jus-tice___ and claim more vic-'tries yet, the earth's our home___ the earth's our own___ there are no bound-'ries with our God, the earth's our home. lai lai lai lai lai lai lai lai lai___ (So)

4. I'll lead all of God's peo-ple in wor-ship and in praise and break the bread of
freedom, the bless-ing cup we'll raise, our dance is strong,___ our dance is long.
In tears we sow, we'll reap with joy, our dance is strong! Lai lai lai lai
lai lai lai lai lai___ (So)

## ✛ Coda

lai lai lai lai      lai lai lai lai lai      lai lai lai lai      lai lai lai lai lai
lai lai lai lai      lai lai lai lai lai

The storyteller circles and skips and plays her tambourine, which is decorated with ribbons. She invites
others to join her freely dancing around the room. On
the lines "We won't go back," arms can be held high
with clenched fists, and pulsate with the beat.

## 9. LITANY RESPONSE

by Colleen Fulmer
© 1986

Send us strength, be our sis-ter _____

Set us free, God our sis-ter _____

Hear our prayer, God our sis-ter _____

## 10. WASHERWOMAN GOD

Do we dare believe in and celebrate a God present with us in ordinary activities, present as much in so-called women's work as in men's, present in sewing, washing, cooking, changing diapers?

During the introduction, march and salute like a soldier then stand in a grandiose, exaggerated pose, pointed up to the almighty transcendent God, the God above us, the warrior God. During the words "But you are...." drop your arms and completely change from grandiose and powerful to simple, warm, and fun-loving.

Chorus: During the first line, bend up and down as if you were scrubbing on a washboard. On "splashing,"

throw up your right arm as if splashing water into the air, on "laughing," throw up your left arm, and wave both arms from side to side on "free."

On the next three lines, pretend to be scrubbing with a mop, then vigorously washing a window. On "Make our hearts...." put both hands over your heart and circle around as if you were scrubbing on a spot. On the last line, scrub on your washboard again and end with both hands on your hips.

Verses: Individuals or groups each take one of the verses and mime the images and activities. All join in dancing the chorus.

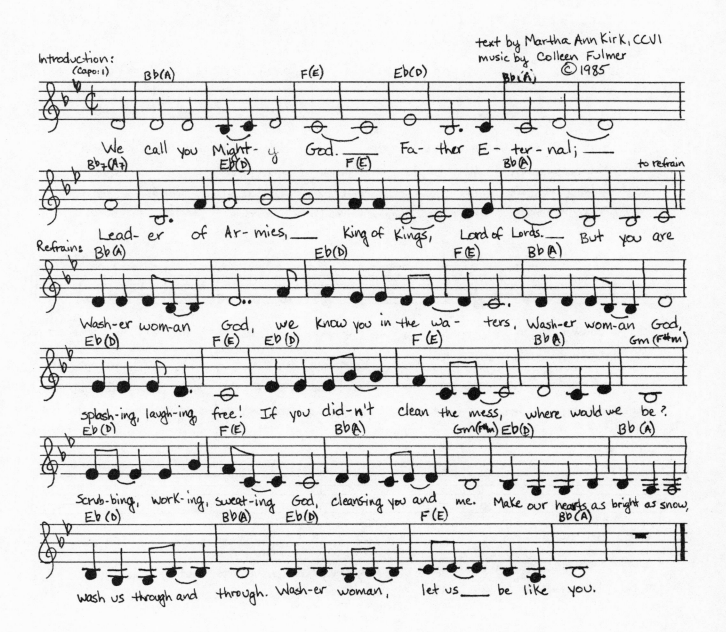

## 11. EL SHADDAI

by Colleen Fulmer
© 1985

Refrain:

El Shad-dai___ Mo-ther who shel-ters___ un-der your wings, In the sweet-ness of life or bit-ter pain.___

1. Do not ask me to leave you I will stay by your side, tender God who cares for the or-phan, who is so long-ing to pro-vide.___ (El Shad-)

2. I will go where you jour-ney___ and our lives will en-twine___ your own peo-ple as my peo-ple, and your God will be mine.___ (El Shad-)

3. Old wo-man, younger daughter,___ Pre-cious wi-dow, or-phan child.___ Mo-ther God who knows all our long-ings, who from the strug-gle births a child.___ (El Shad-)

Get in pairs and stand in a circle. If this is done with fixed chairs or pews, just hold hands and sway during the verses.

Chorus: The left persons from each pair bow their heads to receive blessings. On "*El Shaddai*, mother who shelters...." the right persons slowly lift their right arms out to the side and up and then gently bring them down, placing their right hands on the heads of their partners. On "Under your wings...." they slowly lift their left arms out to the side and up, gently placing their left hands on the heads of their partners.

They hold hands there for a moment, then bring them down, very gently touching the shoulders and arms of the person being blessed. During the next chorus, the persons on the right bow their heads and those on the left bless them. They continue to alternate on each chorus.

Verses: The partners hold both hands, look into each other's eyes, and walk around in a circle.

## 12. PASSIONATE GOD

by Colleen Fulmer
©1985

God is passionate life, Strong and vibrant in us as

We seek
1. jus — tice
2. free- dom
3. e - qua-li - ty
4. digni - ty
5. peace in our day
For all peo - ple.

## 13. JUDGE'S DILEMMA

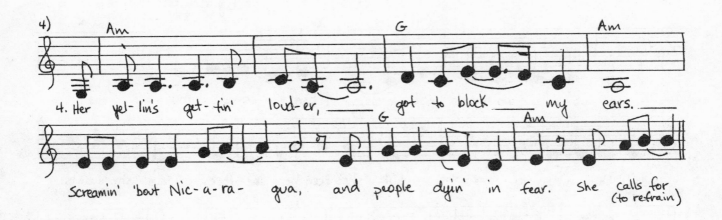

4. Her yel-lin's get-tin' loud-er, _____ got to block _____ my ears. _____
Screamin' 'bout Nic-a-ra- gua, and people dyin' in fear. She calls for
(to refrain)

5. This wid-ow's pound-in hard- er, my bolts and locks_____ won't hold. Her
pray-in'_ makes me ner - vous,_____ makes my blood run cold. For she wants...
(to refrain)

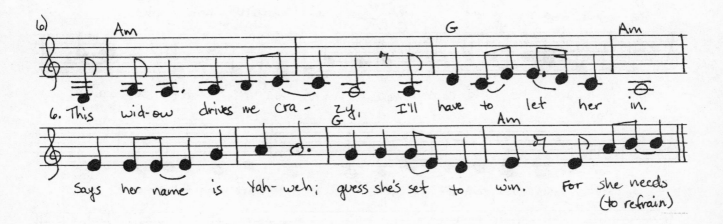

6. This wid-ow drives me cra - zy, I'll have to let her in.
Says her name is Yah-weh; guess she's set to win. For she needs
(to refrain)

## 14. BE NEAR ME, O GOD

by Colleen Fulmer
©1985

## 15. CRY OF RAMAH

by Colleen Fulmer
© 1985

Refrain:

A Voice is heard in Ra-mah, Hir-o-shi-ma, Sal-va-dor; ___
Wo-men re-fus-ing com-fort for their child-ren are no more; ___ no
gar-land of love-ly flo-wers can dis-pel the an-cient grief ___ or
Si-lence the an-guished voic-es that ab-hor the war ma-chine ___

1) 1. If the He-rod in us could be faced and then tamed with com-pas-sion ___
___ all the dark clouds we've cast we'd bind in a mur-mur of peace. ___ (to refrain)

2) 2. If our lea-ders could look in the eyes of the child-ren we car-ry ___
___ they would for-get the bombs they drop and their bud-gets for war. ___ (to refrain)

3. If the na-tions so dis-tant and sep'-rate could break bread to-ge-ther ___ com-ing to know that we are fam-ily with warm hearts to share ___ (to refrain)

4. If the beau-ty of God's cre-a-tion could draw us to won-der ___ hum-bly we'd drop our fears and pride and give birth to new life ___ (to refrain)

A voice was heard in Ramah, wailing and loud lamentation. Rachel weeping for her children, she refused to be consoled, because they are no more (Jer. 31:15; Matt. 2:18)

Ramah was the place of a concentration camp to which the survivors of the destruction of Jerusalem were taken. Poetically, Rachel, the mother of the tribes, is imaged crying for her children who have been lost.

Crying, grieving, and shedding tears are important. If we deny evil or suppress grief or anger, destructive forces can get stronger.

During the words "A voice is heard in Ramah," bend the right elbow and bring the arm up in front of the face, then wipe the back of your hand over your eyes as if wiping away tears, then bring the arm down to the right side. During "Hiroshima, Salvador," bend the left elbow and bring the arm up in front of the face, then wipe the back of your hand over your eyes as if wiping away tears, then bring the arm down to the right side. During "Women refusing comfort," double up your fists and raise your arms above your head, elbows slightly bend allowing yourself to feel anger. During "for their children are no more," open your fingers and bring your arms down showing that you have nothing left in them and slightly bend forward with grief. During "No garland of lovely flowers....," etc., hold hands and sway from side to side. Explain before doing the song that we stand holding hands in solidarity with those who have suffered through the ages and who suffer today. Repeat the movements each time "A voice is heard...." is sung.

## 16. MARTHA'S PROFESSION OF FAITH

This chant may be done slowly and quietly as a meditation with people seated and perhaps swaying from side to side. It can build in tempo and volume and be done standing and holding hands. All sway from side to side. During the part "You are resurrection, you are the life," all slowly raise their arms while swaying. During "You are the Messiah, the Son of God," all slowly lower their arms while swaying.

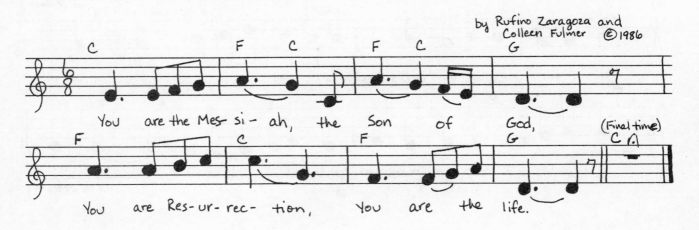

by Rufino Zaragoza and Colleen Fulmer © 1986

You are the Mes-si-ah, the Son of God,

You are Res-ur-rec-tion, You are the life.

## 17. MARY MAGDALENE'S SONG

During "Praise our God who raises us to new life," slowly raise the right arm. During the next line, raise the left arm. On the first Alleluia, both arms come down, and on the second Alleluia, both arms go up. Right at the end, fists should be clenched, then burst open with a pulse of energy.

by Colleen Fulmer
© 1986

Refrain:

Praise our God who rais-es us to new life God who does such

won-ders ___ Al-le-lu - ia, ___ Al-le-lu - ia. ___

1. Praise our God ___ with cym-bals and with strings. Give God glo-ry with voice and tam-bou-rine. (to refrain)

2. Dance for God ___ with flowers and bal-loons. Give God glory with tru-mpet, harp, and flute. (to refrain)

3. Clap your hands, O nations, sing out praise! Give God glory who blesses all our days. (to refrain)

4. Let the drums and timbrel sound our song Give God glory, our hearts will beat as one! (to refrain)

5. Clang-ing cy-mbals that bang and greet the day Clash-ing cy-mbals that clang to praise God's name. (to refrain)

6. Let all peo-ple who breathe re-joice in God who is glory and love for-ev-er more. (to refrain)

## 18. DORCAS' SONG

text by Martha Ann Kirk, C.C.V.I.
music by Colleen Fulmer
© 1986

3. For God has covered Eve with her warm skins, clothes the lil-ies___ in such beau-ty___ our God mends clothes in the de-sert___ and dress-es___ us up in her glo-ry___ (to coda)

This God hears our cries, the wo-men dance, sing-ing "Dor-cas, a-rise!"___ We won't for-get our sis-ters,___ no we wo—n't for-get our sis-ters___ We won't for-get our sis-ters,___ no we wo-n't for-get our sis-ters___

Most of this music may be heard on *Cry of Ramah, Songs and Dances Crying out for Peace and Justice, Celebrating Feminine Images of God,* cassette tape available from the Loretto Spirituality Network, 529 Pomona Ave., Albany, California 94706.

Some of these can be seen on *Daughters Who Image God,* a video tape available from Sheed & Ward, 115 E. Armour Blvd., Kansas City, Mo. 64141-4292.

# Bibliography

Actemeier, Paul. *Mark*. Proclamation Commentaries. Philadelphia: Fortress Press, 1975.

Adams, Doug. *Congregational Dancing in Christian Worship*. Austin, TX: Sharing Co., 1971.

_____.*Humor in the American Pulpit from George Whitefield Through Henry Ward Beecher*. North Aurora, IL: Sharing Co., 1975.

Aune, David E. *Prophesy in Early Christianity and the Ancient Mediterranean World*. Grand Rapids, MI: Eerdmans, 1983.

Braverman, Jan. *Jerome's Commentary on Daniel: A Study of Comparative Jewish and Christian Interpretations of the Hebrew Bible*. Washington, DC: Catholic Biblical Association of America, 1978.

Brooten, Bernadette. *Women Leaders in the Ancient Synagogue*. Chico, CA: Scholars Press, 1982.

Brown, Raymond E., S.S. *The Anchor Bible, the Gospel According to John* (xiii-xxi), vol. 29a. Garden City, NY: Doubleday, 1970.

_____.*The Community of the Beloved Disciple*. New York: Paulist Press, 1979.

Cannon, Katie Geneva. "The Emergence of Black Feminist Consciousness." In *Feminist Interpretation of the Bible*, pp. 30-40. Edited by Letty M. Russell. Philadelphia: Westminster Press, 1985.

Chicago, Judy. *Embroidering Our Heritage, The Dinner Party Needlework*. Garden City, NY: Anchor Books, 1980.

Chittister, Joan, OSB. *Winds of Change; Women Challenge the Church*. Kansas City, Mo.: Sheed & Ward, 1986.

Christ, Carol P. *Diving Deep and Surfacing, Women Writers on Spiritual Quest*. Boston: Beacon Press, 1980.

Dobson, James C. *Straight Talk to Men and Their Wives*. Waco, TX: Word, 1980.

Eliade, Mircea. *Rites and Symbols of Initiation*. Translated by Willard R. Trask. New York: Harper Torchbooks, 1958.

Exum, Cheryl J. "'Mother in Israel': A Familiar Figure Reconsidered." In *Feminist Interpretation of the Bible*, pp. 73-85. Edited by Letty M. Russell. Philadelphia: Westminster Press, 1985.

Fiorenza, Elisabeth Schussler. *Bread Not Stone, the Challenge of Feminist Biblical Interpretation*. Boston: Beacon Press, 1984.

_____.*In Memory of Her, a Feminist Theological Reconstruction of Christian Origins*. New York: Crossroads, 1983.

Fortune, Marie Marshall. *Sexual Violence, the Unmentionable Sin*. New York: Pilgrim Press, 1983.

Frye, L. Thomas, ed. *American Quilts: A Handmade Legacy*. Oakland, CA: The Oakland Museum, 1981.

Goldberg, Herb. *The Hazards of Being Male: Surviving the Myth of Masculine Privilege*. New York: New American Library, 1976.

Haechen, Ernest. *The Acts of the Apostles, a Commentary*. Philadelphia: Westminster Press, 1971.

Hoppin, Ruth. *Priscilla, Author of the Epistle to the Hebrews*. New York: Exposition Press, 1969.

Hunter, Edwina and Wilson, Beclee Newcomer. "Celebration of the Inclusive Language Lectionary." *Journal of Women and Religion* 3 (Summer 1984): 5-11.

Hunter, Edwina. "Reflections on the *Christa*." *Journal of Women and Religion* 4 (Winter 1985).

Hurty, Kathleen. "Power in a New Key: Excerpts from Purdue." *Concern* 28 (January 1986):36-37.

*The Jerusalem Bible*. Garden City, N.Y.: Doubleday and Co., 1966.

Kirk, Martha Ann, CCVI *Dancing with Creation: Mexican and Native American Dance in Christian Worship and Education*. Saratoga, CA: Resource Publications, 1983.

_____."Dancing Away Power Structures." *National Catholic Reporter*, 28 October 1983, p. 10.

Kokopeli, Bruce, and Lakey, George. "More Power Than We Want: Masculine Sexuality and Violence." *Reweaving the Web of Life: Feminism and Nonviolence*, pp. 231-240. Edited by Pam McAllister. Philadelphia: New Society Publishers, 1982.

Lacks, Roslyn. *Women and Judaism, Myth, History, and Struggle*. Garden City, NY: Doubleday, 1980.

Lark Books Staff, and Philban, Marianne, eds. *The Ribbon, a Celebration of Life*. Asheville, NC: Lark Books, 1985.

LaVerdiere, Eugene. *The New Testament in the Life of the Church*. Notre Dame: Ave Maria Press, 1980.

McDonald, Denis R. *The Legend and the Apostle: The Battle for Paul in Story and Canon*. Philadelphia: Westminster Press, 1983.

Mead, Margaret. *Male and Female: A Study of the Sexes in a Changing World*. New York: Morrow Paperback, William Morrow & Co., 1949, 1975).

Mollenkott, Virginia Ramsey. *The Divine Feminine: The Biblical Imagery of God as Female*. New York: Crossroad, 1983.

Moltmann-Wendel, Elisabeth. *The Women Around Jesus: Reflections on Authentic Personhood*. Translated by J. Bowden. New York: Crossroad, 1982.

Moore, Carey A. *Daniel, Esther, Jeremiah: The Additions, the Anchor Bible*. Garden City, NY: Doubleday, 1977.

Moynahan, Michael E., S.J. *Once Upon a Parable*. New York: Paulist Press, 1984.

*The New American Bible*. New York: Thomas Nelson, Publishers, 1970.

Nunnally-Cox, Janice. *Foremothers, Women of the Bible*. New York: Seabury, 1981.

Otwell, John H. *And Sarah Laughed: The Status of Women in the Old Testament*. Philadelphia: Westminster Press, 1977.

Pagels, Elaine. "To The Universe Belong the Dancer," *Parabola, Myth and Quest for Meaning*, (May 1979): 6-9.

Quinney, Valerie. "Textile Women: Three Generations in the Mill." *Southern Exposure* 34 (Winter 1976):66-72.

Riley, Maria. "Women Workers in The Global Factor." *Center Focus* no. 52 (January 1983): 3.

Ruether, Rosemary Radford. "Mothers of the Church: Ascetic Women in the Late Patristic Age." In *Women of Spirit, Female Leadership in the Jewish and Christian Traditions*, pp. 72-98. Edited by Rosemary Radford Ruether and Eleanor McLaughlin. New York: Simon & Schuster, 1979.

_____.*Religion and Sexism*. New York: Simon & Schuster, 1974.

_____.*Sexism and God-Talk*. Boston: Beacon Press, 1983.

Russell, Letty M., ed. *Feminist Interpretation of the Bible*. Philadelphia: Westminster Press, 1985.

Sawicki, Marianne. *Faith and Sexism*. New York: Seabury Press, 1979.

Schneiders, Sandra M., I.H.M. "Women in the Fourth Gospel and the Role of Women in the Contemporary Church." *Biblical Theology Bulletin* 7 (April 1982):35-45.

Sivard, Ruth Leger. *Woman.... A World Survey*. Washington, DC: World Priorities, 1985.

Stagg, Evelyn; and Stagg, Frank. *Women in the World of Jesus*. Philadelphia: Westminster Press, 1978.

Swidler, Leonard J. *Biblical Affirmations of Women*. Philadelphia: Westminster Press, 1979.

Teubal, Savina J. *Sarah The Priestess, the First Matriarch of Genesis*. Athens, OH: Swallow Press, Ohio University Press, 1984.

Theissen, Gerd. *Miracle Stories of the Early Christian Tradition*. Translated by Francis McDonagh. Edinburgh, Scotland: T. & T. Clark, 1982.

Thistlethwaite, Susan Brooks. "Every Two Minutes: Battered Women and Feminist Interpretation." *Feminist Interpretation of the Bible*. Edited by Letty M. Russell. Philadelphia: Westminster Press, 1985.

Tolbert, Mary Ann, ed. *The Bible and Feminist Hermeneutics*. (Semia 28). Baltimore, MD: Scholars Press, 1984.

Trible, Phyllis. "Depatriarchalizing in Biblical Interpretation." *Journal of the American Academy of Religion* 41 (1973):30-48.

_____.God and the Rhetoric of Sexuality. Philadelphia: Fortress Press, 1978.

_____.*Texts of Terror, Literary-Feminist Readings of Biblical Narratives*. Philadelphia: Fortress Press, 1984.

Turner, Victor. *The Ritual Process, Structures and Anti-Structure*. Ithaca, NY: Cornell Paperbacks, 1969.

Ullman, Liv. "Forward." In *Women...A World Survey*, p. 3. Edited by Ruth Leger Sivard. Washington, DC: World Priorities, 1985.

United Nations. "State of the World's Women 1985." *Global Pages* 3 (August/September 1985) :5.

Waetjen, Herman. *The Origin and Destiny of Humanness, an Interpretation of the Gospel According to Matthew*, Corte Madera, CA: Omega Books, 1976.

Weinstein, Matt, and Goodman, Joel. *Playfair, Everybody's Guide to Noncompetitive Play*. Impacet Publishers, 1980.

Wire, Antoinette Clark. "The Miracle Story as the Whole Story." *Southeast Asia Journal of Theology* 22 (1981):29-37.

_____."The Structure of the Gospel Miracle Stories and Their Tellers." *Semia* 11-12(1978):83-113.

Zannotti, Barbara. "Is Peace Possible in a Patriarchal Society?" *Probe* 6 (October/November 1982):1-2.